CONCILIUM

CONCILIUM
ADVISORY COMMITTEE

Gregory Baum	Montreal/QC. Canada
José Oscar Beozzo	São Paulo, SP Brazil
Wim Beuken	Louvain, Belgium
Leonardo Boff	Petrópolis, Brazil
John Coleman	Los Angeles, CA. USA
Norbert Greinacher	Tübingen, Germany
Gustavo Gutiérrez	Lima, Peru
Hermann Häring	Tübingen, Germany
Werner G. Jeanrond	Oslo, Norway
Jean-Pierre Jossua	Paris, France
Maureen Junker-Kenny	Dublin, Ireland
François Kabasele Lumbala	Kinshasa, Rep. Dem. Congo
Nicholas Lash	Cambridge, UK
Mary-John Mananzan	Manila, The Philippines
Alberto Melloni	Reggio, Emilia Italy
Norbert Mette	Münster, Germany
Dietmar Mieth	Tübingen, Germany
Jürgen Moltmann	Tübingen, Germany
Teresa Okure	Port Harcourt, Nigeria
Aloysius Pieris	Kelaniya/Colombo, Sri Lanka
Giuseppe Ruggieri	Catania, Italy
Paul Schotsmans	Louvain, Belgium
Janet Martin Soskice	Cambridge, UK
Elsa Tamez	San José, Costa Rica
Christoph Theobald	Paris, France
David Tracy	Chicago, Ill. USA
Marciano Vidal	Madrid, Spain
Ellen van Wolde	Tilburg, The Netherlands
Johannes Zizioulas	Pergamo, Turkey
Regina Ammicht Quinn	Tübingen Germany
Hille Haker	Chicago, USA
Jon Sobrino	San Salvador, El Salvador
Luiz Carlos Susin	Porto Alegre, Brazil
Silvia Scatena	Bologna, Italy
Susan A. Ross	USA, Los Angeles
Solange Lefebvre	Montreal/QC. Canada
Erik Borgman	Amsterdam, Netherlands
Andres Torres Queiruga	Santiago, Spain

CONCILIUM   2019/5

Queer Theologies: Becoming the Queer Body of Christ

Edited by

Stefanie Knauss and Carlos Mendoza-Álvarez

Published in 2019 by SCM Press, 3rd Floor, Invicta House, 108–114 Golden Lane, London EC1Y 0TG.

SCM Press is an imprint of Hymns Ancient & Modern Ltd (a registered charity) 13A Hellesdon Park Road, Norwich NR6 5DR, UK

Copyright © International Association of Conciliar Theology, Madras (India)

www.concilium.in

English translations copyright © 2019 Hymns Ancient & Modern Ltd.

All rights reserved. No part of this publication may be reproduced, stored in a retrieval system, or transmitted, in any form or by any means, electronic, mechanical, photocopying or otherwise, without the prior written permission of the Board of Directors of Concilium.

ISBN 978-0-334-03151-2

Concilium is published in March, June, August, October, December

Contents

Editorial 7

Part One: Foundations
As Queer as it Gets
ANDRÉ S. MUSSKOPF 13

Constructive Theological Perspectives: What is Queer Theology?
SUSANNAH CORNWALL 22

Part Two: Experiences
Queer is God
MURPH MURPHY 35

The Will of God
FR. PAUL UCHECHUKWU 39

Letter From a Reluctant Indian
LUKAS AVENDAÑO 43

Part Three: Theologies
Queering Jewish Theology in Parables
GWYNN KESSLER 51

The Multiple Bodies of Jesus
CARMENMARGARITA SÁNCHEZ DE LÉON 61

Ecclesiology: Becoming the Queer, Postcolonial,
(Eco-)feminist Body of Christ in Asia
SHARON A. BONG 70

'Can Anything Good Come from Nazareth? Come and See!'
An Invitation to Dialogue Between Queer Theories and
African Theologies
NONTANDO HADEBE   81

Love in the Last Days: The Eschatological Marking of Bodies
Resembling an Infinitely Queer Desire
ÁNGEL F. MÉNDEZ-MONTOYA   91

Queer Liturgy
MARILÚ ROJAS SALAZAR   100

A Queer (Beginning to the) Bible
GERALD O. WEST AND CHARLENE VAN DER WALT   109

Queer Muslim Theologies
SHANON SHAH   119

Part Four: Theological Forum
Exiles in the Global Village and Political Compassion
CONRADO ZEPEDA MIRAMONTES SJ   133

The Imperative of Reforestation in Fighting Climate Change in Asia
REYNALDO D. RALUTO   137

Contributors   142

Editorial

Queer Theories and Theologies

Queer theology – what is that? What does it do? And how can we imagine the body of Christ as 'queer'? These are some of the questions we pursue in this volume.

Queer theologies are inspired by the critical analysis of queer theory which has emerged in the late 20th century from the experiences of subjects and subjectivities who are marginalized because of their non-normative sexuality (gay, lesbian, bisexual) or gender identity (trans, intersexual, non-binary). As André Musskopf's introductory article shows, queer theory began by questioning the assumption of identity categories such as gender or sexuality as natural and unchangeable. Drawing on Michel Foucault and deconstructionist theories, queer theorists[1] argue that the processes of naturalization of socially constructed binary categories are not disinterested but serve to maintain political power relationships, capitalist structures, patriarchy and epistemological systems. Whereas the fantasy of natural, stable identities provides the foundation for the construction of hierarchies and systems of oppression and exploitation, shifting and unstable identities are perceived as a threat: they 'trouble' the status quo and those who benefit from it. As a bridge between the academic realm, social movements and concrete social and political issues, queer theory has always been a theoretical as well as political project in its concerns for marginalized bodies that suffer from physical, epistemological, political and psychological violence. This is also noticeable today, when queer theory's critical 'undoing' of categories of difference, processes of othering and relationships of oppression expands from the focus on gender and sexuality in the west to the epistemic south to include ethnicity, race, class, disability and other categories used to classify and marginalize individuals in their intersectional interactions within the broader context of the decolonial project.[2]

Queer theory has thus made important contributions to understanding the entanglement of identities, desires, ways of knowing, politics, economies, and not least, religions. And this is where queer theologies begin their critical and constructive work. Susannah Cornwall's contribution provides an overview of the field, some of its results and the challenges it faces for its future work.[3] For queer theologies, the experience of oppression of LGBTIQ+ persons in church and society is a performative influence, and thus we include in this issue the testimonials of three individuals, Murph Murphy, Fr. Paul Uchechukwu and Lukas Avendaño, who defy western normative categories of gender, sexuality and spirituality. Courageously, they speak of their struggles, the oppression they faced in their communities, and the spiritual depths they discovered in themselves. Departing from such experiences, queer theologies question the role of religion and theology in supporting structures of oppression based on binary categories, such as sex, gender or race.[4] How have theologies, through their concepts and doctrines, supported or even enabled marginalization and oppression? How do ideas about God impact social structures? How does christology legitimize a culture of violence, racism and patriarchy? How do eschatological visions inhibit the good life of all *now*? How have liturgies cemented hierarchies and exclusion? In this volume, Gwynn Kessler, Sharon Bong, Ángel Méndez-Montoya and Marilú Rojas offer a queer critique of these and other issues and constructively develop creative visions of other possibilities.

Queer theologies critique the theoretical and methodological assumptions of the theological project, and encourage an attitude of humility in the awareness of the fluidity not just of identity categories, but of theology itself. While always searching for God's truth, theologies will never quite achieve it, and thus in order to approach it as closely as possible, they will have to shift and change, and to be open to the ever-new reality of God Godself. Rather than focusing on meaning or being, on trying to grasp a truth and hold on to it, queer theologies think in terms of doing, becoming, desiring and living the sometimes confusing entanglements of bodies, concepts and actions. Methodologically speaking, this reflects in the emphasis on concrete, embodied experience as a source of theology, attention to the theological significance of creativity, narrative and practice, and to theologies that happen outside of the realm of academia, as we see in the contributions by Carmen Margarita Sanchez De León, Gerald West and Charlene van der Welt, Nontando Hadebe and others in this issue.

One of the various meanings of 'to queer' is 'to transgress', and queer theologies are transgressive in many ways: in their critique of traditions, norms and authorities, in their persistent yet ever fallible and insufficient pursuits of the divine, in their move beyond the academic ivory tower, in their political and social engagement, in their openness towards the wisdom of bodies and desires, and not least, in their transgression of boundaries between denominations and religions as they rediscover the living power of spiritualities. Kessler's analysis of rabbinic parables as spaces of fluid imaginations of gender, and Shah's post-colonial discussion of queer Muslim theologies as contestations of power and politics offer just two examples of the fruitful encounters among queer theologies in all religious and spiritual traditions.

Today, queer theologies are challenged by the recognition of the intersectionality of various factors of discrimination such as race, class or ability, and the opening up towards a global horizon in the decolonial project. The articles gathered here make important contributions to both these issues as they engage in a dialogue with queer, post-colonial and decolonial theories in the attempt to not only understand better the realities of oppression from which they emerge, but also contribute to the transformation of the world so that all may live and flourish.

As the articles collected here show, becoming the queer body of Christ is an eschatological path that queer theologies have been exploring in the midst of systemic violence. To lovingly re-member the bodies and territories dis-membered by global violence is an expression of the messianic times. The bodies that really matter, the exploited and invisible bodies of LGBTIQ+ persons, migrants, disappeared people, persons with different abilities, are today the living members of the queer body of Christ. Their multiple resistances, struggles for dignity, life and hope represent a precious dimension of the eschatological process of redemption.

Finally, the two contributions to the Theological Forum, by Reynaldo Raluto and Conrado Zepeda Miramontes, do not employ queer theory or methodology, but they are also motivated by the concern with social justice that characterizes queer theologies and respond to the challenge of those suffering bodies that matter to God, and that are also calling to all of us. Zepeda offers a brief discussion of the phenomenon of migration,

Editorial

especially in the Latin American context, and the idea of political compassion, whereas Raluto thinks about deforestation as ecological sin and the ways in which some Asian communities draw on the sacrament of reconciliation to encourage ecological reparations.

Stefanie Knauss and Carlos Mendoza-Álvarez

Notes

1. Some formative authors in the field have been Teresa de Lauretis, Eve Kosofsky Sedgwick and Judith Butler.
2. For a discussion of decolonial queer theory and additional bibliography, see Pedro Paulo Gomes Pereira, 'Reflecting on Decolonial Queer', *GLQ: A Journal of Lesbian and Gay Studies*, 25.3 (2019), 403–429.
3. In addition to the rich bibliography in Cornwall's contribution, see for a recent, accessible introduction Linn Marie Tonstad, *Queer Theology: Beyond Apologetics*, Eugene: Cascade, 2018.
4. For a focus on gay and lesbian sexualities, see the *Concilium* issue on *Homosexualities* (1/2008).

Part One: Foundations

As Queer as it Gets

ANDRÉ S. MUSSKOPF

Queer theory or queer studies emerged in the 1990s in a particular context but with implications in different fields of knowledge and with new ways of articulating issues of sex, gender and sexuality. This article reconstructs the historical emergence and developments of such studies, their relation to political activism and to new ways of looking at issues of identity. It discusses the use of the term/concept 'queer' and related terms/concepts used in other contexts and the implications of the theoretical and methodological proposals connected to it. It is intended to be a brief introduction to the presentation and discussions in the field of theology, and its appropriation and use in the so-called 'queer theologies.

It is very common that articles or reflections on queer theory, studies, theology/ies start and work with a play on words and expressions. Although 'queer' as a term is not actually translatable to other languages (at least not with the same meaning and not with the same social, historical and political content), its 'strangeness' in relation to cultural norms regarding sex, gender and sexuality allows for multiple appropriations and developments. This play, twist, pun with words and expressions is part of the epistemology and method involved in dealing with those norms, their meanings and their consequences in social life (both individually and collectively), precisely because language is performance,[1] at the same time reflecting and constructing this same social order. This 'practice' is rooted in camp, usually understood as a particular kind of humour exercised as a form of subversion in LGBTIQ+[2] cultures, but also in the anger and frustration rising from the lack of intentions or possibilities to conform to socially accepted norms – precisely for its 'strangeness'. In this way, subverting language and its norms, which at the same time points to the very concrete social and cultural practices that are imbedded in such language, creates a space in which the known is made strange and/or defamiliarized and it is necessary to reorganize and resignify reality. Because it is an open and unpredictable process, the responses and consequences to 'queer' (or the act of 'queering') vary immensely, both in terms of rejection of the mere idea of interrogations of that which is considered 'given', 'natural' or 'normal', including violence (at an individual level such as violence directed at LGBTIQ+ people, but also collectively in conservative and fascist movements currently rising all over the world with their conscious aim at issues of sex, gender and sexuality), and in terms of new possible arrangements and understandings, or at least new meanings and social implications of such arrangements that are not necessarily so new or original. This is as queer as it gets!

II The emergence of 'queer'

Although language plays an important role in those issues and debates, thus the 'queer' noun-verb-adjective (queers queer queering), its emergence and use in both political and theoretical contexts points to the materiality of life, relationships and practices which through their very existence question modern assumptions of universality, stability and linearity. There is no queer theory, studies, theology/ies without the concrete lives and experiences of multiple subjects in relation to sex, gender and sexuality as political statements against dogmatic and normative ordering forces and, more specifically, outside of the diverse forms of direct political organization and intervention in different social spheres. In the genealogy of the use of 'queer'[3] in terms of individual and collective identification, political action and theoretical reflection, the subjective and social identities of the 'queer subjects', their impact as a dis/organized collective and the knowledge produced in relation to those experiences and practices are intimately connected and also entail an epistemological claim. There is no neutral, objective and impartial assessment of reality and its reflection as assumed in modern positivism, but only committed engagement, with the critical and creative potential of acknowledging and embracing the different levels and places of situatedness.[4] It is a matter of bodies that matter, their locations, their relations and the meanings and values that emerge from them.[5]

The use of the term 'queer' to express such identities and identifications, political action through social movements and theoretical reflections arises from the appropriation of a word used to describe and discriminate against people who do not fit the hetero/normative rules in terms of sex, gender and sexuality. Taken from its original meaning as 'strange', 'odd', 'eccentric' it has been used in English-speaking contexts since the end of the 1980s and early 1990s to refer to LGBTIQ+ people and their 'strange' and 'out of the norm' experiences, both in social movements and by scholars in relation to the term 'homosexuality' (questioning the very idea of 'homosexual' as medical category created in the 1860s which established the hetero-homo oppositional binary opening the way for some kind of 'acceptance' and 'normativization' of homosexuality – so-called homonormativity, a specific and socially accepted way of being 'homosexual') and in the field of Gay and Lesbian Studies (questioning the assimilationist perspective of an essentialist identity focus, seeing identity as stable and inflexible, although differing one from the other). In this sense, the term 'queer' is used to include different perspectives and experiences being taken by some scholars as an umbrella term for multiple realities and their interconnections and intersections or, as Eve K. Sedgwick states: 'the open mesh of possibilities, gaps, overlaps, dissonances and resonances, lapses and excesses of meaning when the constituent elements of anyone's gender, of anyone's sexuality aren't made (or can't be made) to signify monolithically.'[6]

One of the issues that influenced and marked the emergence of such a perspective was the HIV/AIDS epidemic in the 1980s, when it hit northern (American and European) countries, although it is known today that it was actually impacting African countries much before that. According to Tamsin Spargo:

'With the onset of AIDS, this already fractured collective was confronted by a new set of pressures. The popular discourses that misrepresented AIDS as a gay disease contributed to renewed homophobia and necessitated a review of assimilationist strategies. Acceptance was all too quickly revealed to be tolerance, which was swiftly becoming intolerance. This led, in turn, to a renewed but decentralized radicalism in gay and lesbian politics. New coalitions were formed between men and women, not on the basis of essential identity but of a shared commitment to resisting the representations that were costing the lives of those with AIDS. [...] It was in the context of AIDS activism and rejection of assimilationist strategies that "queer" was redeployed in its current fashion both in popular culture and in theory.'[7]

This kind of activism was embodied by organizations such as ACT-UP and Queer Nation. The use of the term 'queer' to characterize this renewal in the political movement represents a strategy and methodology that were articulated theoretically in the 1990s. The main focus is to subvert the categories constructed through medicalization in order to resignify terms and adjectives previously used to stigmatize. Appearing for the first time in works by Teresa de Lauretis, Eve K. Sedgwick and Judith Butler, this term was incorporated in the debates in Gay and Lesbian Studies, representing a theoretical perspective that surpasses and breaks away from the binary identity categories constructed and maintained by social movements and academics. It is not restricted to the process of the construction of identities related to sex, gender and sexuality, but is concerned with the multiple intersections of those with other markers, such as race and ethnicity, class, belief etc. Besides queer activism, feminist theories, the paradigm shift in historical and sociological studies in the context of post-structuralism, including especially the work of Michel Foucault, all influenced this new theoretical (and political) perspective. According to William B. Turner: '"Queer" has the virtue of offering, in the context of academic inquiry into gender identity and sexual identity, a relatively novel term that connotes etymologically a crossing of boundaries but that refers to nothing in particular, thus leaving the question of its denotations open to contest and revision'.[8]

III 'Queer' in context
The word 'queer', as seen, refers to a very concrete and specific context (geographically, culturally and historically). Although it has been appropriated in other contexts and languages using the English word (so much as to become part of the common vocabulary, mostly in academic settings, but in some cases also in the context of social movements and current common language), in other contexts other words or concepts have been used to reflect and align or be identified as aligned with the discussions and political actions in this field. In Spanish, for example, some have used

the word *torcida* ('twisted')[9] to name this kind of reflection, with not much success or correspondence in social movements or research. In my own work, I have used the word *'viadagem'* ('faggotting'),[10] and although this word (*'viado'*, a derogatory slang term for male homosexuals) is more or less used and rejected by LGBTIQ+ groups and movements (just as 'queer' is in English speaking contexts), it cannot be taken as a translation or as a term that encompasses the multiple and open meanings projected by the word 'queer', especially in its specific relation to queer men's experience (not necessarily only gay, but also transvestites and trans men). There are many other words and concepts in different contexts and languages that are used or can be used to relate to the concept, method and theory expressed by 'queer', partially, completely or differently. One of the things that they do have in common and that puts them in the same conceptual, theoretical and political framework is the subversion or perversion of what are understood to be traditional (medicalized and naturalized) norms regarding sex, gender and sexuality, mostly reclaiming hateful and derogatory words, expressions and symbols and using them against themselves in a positive, assertive and affirmative way and, precisely for that, causing discomfort, destabilizing their usual meaning and the power relations that support their use as weapons against LGBTIQ+ people and communities.

So, putting the issue of finding the correct or better word or expression (in English or in any other language) aside, the main issue is the critical reflection on how sex, gender and sexuality are constructed and the power relations that derive from the categorization and intelligibility of some assumed identities or identifications (for example, the heterosexual masculine male in relation to all other possible experiences and meanings that do not fit this paradigm). In her theological reflection from a Latin American perspective, Marcella Althaus-Reid has used the concept of 'indecency' to refer to a 'counter-discourse for the unmasking and unclothing of the sexual assumptions built into Liberation Theology during the past decades but also today when confronting issues of globalization and the new neo-liberal world order. Indecency as a social gesture is extremely political and erotic, and relates to the construction of the identity of the subject through the subversion of economic, religious and sexual identities.'[11] In relation to theology, she states:

'Indecent Theology is a theology which problematizes and undresses the mythical layers of multiple oppression in Latin America, a theology which, finding its point of departure at the crossroads of Liberation Theology and Queer Thinking, will reflect on economic and theological oppression with passion and imprudence. An Indecent Theology will question the traditional Latin American field of decency and order as it permeates and supports the multiple (ecclesiological, theological, political and amatory) structures of life in my country, Argentina, and in my continent.'[12]

IV Queer at work

Naming is itself (at the level of personal or individual identification, organized social movements and/or academic and theoretical reflection) an epistemological issue, although also a political and contextual one. In many cases, identifying oneself, one's political action and academic work as 'queer' might be a strategy to align with a larger community, political and theoretical movement. In other cases, using local and native terms and concepts is a way not only to translate (as seen above, translatability is hardly possible in this case), but to think about issues related to sex, gender and sexuality and their relation to other identity and social markers and processes and to enrich the conversations with elements that are particular to a specific context (especially in a post-colonial and decolonial perspective). In this sense, 'queer' (as an identity marker and as a theoretical framework) should not be imposed on the analysis of and reflection about any given situation and context, although it can also be a useful perspective to engage in such analysis and reflections, also when considering different historical and contextual experiences. That's why it is possible, in theological and religious reflections, to talk about a 'queer Jesus', or 'queer subjects and identities in the Bible'[13] (or other sacred texts, narratives, rituals), even if this twentieth-century concept is strange to those contexts. 'Queer' is, then, a lens or an analytical category that can be used to analyse, describe and understand social, cultural, political and religious dynamics and their impacts in their own contexts and in our own.

Taking as a point of departure the idea (and reality) of sexuality as a fluid, complex and multiple experience, and not a given one as usually is assumed, queer studies 'interrogate aspects of social life – the family, intimate relationships – but also look at places not typically thought of as sexualized – the economy, for example.'[14] Following Foucault's proposals, they show how categories are constructed and attributed according to power relations and add the realities of sex, gender and sexuality to the discussion and investigation of issues and situations in which they are usually not engaged with, proving that 'the personal life is sexualized – and heterosexualized.'[15] Those are the lenses that queer scholars use to develop their work. What queer studies propose (and do) is to turn sex, gender and sexuality into subjects for academic work in the investigation of every aspect and area of life. According to Rachel E. Poulsen: 'Because society is organized on a heterosexual model, challenging the presumptive claims of heteronormativity forces the questioning of the logic of government, religion, medicine, law, and every discipline that structures people's lives'.[16] In this sense, according to William B. Turner, it also questions 'the scholarly ideal of dispassionate reflection, with reason as one's only guide, [which] entails a refusal to recognize the multiple ways in which cultural and psychological factors influence what we think and write'.[17]

Stephen D. Moore argues that queer theory or queer studies, more than a closed set of theories and concepts is a sensibility in relation to reality that is, in fact, queer.[18] It is an oppositional perspective since its reflection is centred in the opposition to that which is taken as absolute norm, revealing, through a methodological sensibility, that identity itself is 'queer' and does not necessarily follow models or patterns, opening the possibilities for other identities to exist, be acknowledged and valued as a source for political and academic work. So, queer theory, studies, theology/is are, before anything, a political action as all knowledge is related to power. They indicate new ways of reflecting, or at least new ways of looking at existing categories and concepts to question if and how they continue to be relevant and for whom.

V Theologically queer
In the production of queer theologies there is no fixed place, no closed space, no stable belonging. In each step, the condition of foreigner is evident, the condition of the one who is not in their place and who makes each place their own, open to communication, hybridization, entanglement, syncretism. It is 'diaspora as a choice, as a need to transit, transposition of borders [...]. Diaspora as a desire for self-modification in one's own and other psycho-geographical spaces.'[19] This permanent condition of being

a foreigner in a strange land, with its surprises, violence and pleasures, defines the forms of theological discourse. Diaspora is the place where the questions emerge, which evokes provisional answers and designs a project of queer theologies affirming a positionality that resists to a heterocentric order of theological knowledge. That's why:

'Queer theologies are usually biographical theologies. One needs to follow that diasporic movement which allows us to understand the paths crossed, and the ways in which theological identities are still challenged, transformed, retracted and disguised in Christianity. [...] Queer theologies go into diasporas by using tactics of temporary occupation; disruptive practices which are not necessarily to be repeated, and reflections which aim to be disconcerting.'[20]

Notes

1. Judith Butler, *Lenguagje, poder e identidade*, Madrid: Síntesis, 1997.
2. The acronym varies. In this form it stands for Lesbian, Gay, Bisexual, Transgender, Transsexual, Intersexual, Queer and other non-heteronormative identifications in terms of sex, gender and sexuality. The changes in the acronym express the continuous struggle and search for visibility of different social groups and their experiences. Being identity-based, the different identities, identifications and experiences expressed by the different forms of the acronym cannot be equaled with 'queer' (as 'queer' also appears in some versions of it, like the one being used here, for an identity among others).
3. William B. Turner, *A Genealogy of Queer Theory*, Philadelphia: Temple University Press, 2000.
4. Donna Haraway, 'Saberes localizados: a questão da ciência para o feminismo e o privilégio da perspectiva parcial', *cadernos pagu*, 5 (1995), 7-41.
5. Judith Butler, *Bodies That Matter*, Routledge: New York, 1993.
6. Eve K. Sedgwick, *Tendencies*, Durkham: Duke University Press, 1993, p. 8.
7. Tamsin Spargo, *Foucault and Queer Theory*, Cambridge: Icon, 1999, pp. 34–35, 36.
8. Turner, *A Genealogy of Queer Theory*, p. 35.
9. Ricardo Llamas, *Teoría torcida*, Madrid: Siglo XXI de España Editores, 1998. Also Marcela Althaus-Reid, 'De la Teología de la Liberación Feminista a La Teología Torcida', in Nancy Cardoso, Edla Eggert and André S. Musskopf (eds.), *A graça do mundo transforma deus*, Porto Alegre: Editora Universitária Metodista, 2005, pp. 64–69.
10. André S. Musskopf, *Via(da)gens teológicas*, São Paulo: Fonte Editorial, 2012. A first essay using this idea in dialogue with Frida Kahlo's painting *La venadita*, and the relations between the 'deer-animal' and the 'deer-homosexual/queer', since the word *viado* ('faggot') is related to the word *veado* ('deer'), the later one used to symbolize queer men, is André S. Musskopf, 'Veadagens teológicas', in Edla Eggert (ed.), *[Re]leituras de Frida Kahlo*, Sabta Cruz do Sul: EDUNISC, 2008, pp. 101–120.

11. Marcella Althaus-Reid, *Indecent Theology*, London: Routledge, 2001, p. 168.
12. Althaus-Reid, *Indecent Theology*, p. 2.
13. See Nancy Wilson, *Our Tribe*, New Mexico: Alamo Square Press, 2000; Robert Goss, *Queering Christ*, Cleveland: The Pilgrim Press, 2002.
14. Arlene Stein and Ken Plummer, 'I Can't Even Think Straight', in Steven Seidman (ed.), *Queer Theory/Sociology*, Oxford: Blackwell Publishers, 1996, p. 135.
15. Stein and Plummer, 'I Can't Even Think Straight', p. 135.
16. Rachel E. Poulsen, 'Queer Studies', in Timothy F. Murphy (ed.), *Readers' Guide to Lesbian and Gay Studies*, Chicago: Fitzroy Deadborn, 2000, p. 490.
17. Turner, *A Genealogy of Queer Theory*, p. 5.
18. Stephen D. Moore, *God's Beauty Parlor*, Stanford: Stanford University Press, 2001, p. 18.
19. Massimo Canevacci, *Sincretismos*, São Paulo: Studio Nobel, Instituto Italiano di Cultura, Instituto Cultural Ítalo-Brasileiro, 1996, p. 7 (my translation).
20. Marcella Althaus-Reid, *The Queer God*, London: Routledge, 2003, p. 8.

Constructive Theological Perspectives: What is Queer Theology?

SUSANNAH CORNWALL

Queer is sometimes used as a synonym for LGBT identities, and sometimes as a signal of rejection of identity of all kinds. Queer theologies fall into two main streams, liberationist and subversive, and often involve a thoroughgoing disruption of norms of all kinds, asking questions about power, language, and the limits of identity. Queer theologians and interpreters re-read and re-frame aspects of biblical, historical, moral, pastoral, doctrinal, systematic and constructive Christian theology in light of queer people's lives, concerns and politics. This includes intersectional reflection on ethnicity, disability, class and socio-economic location.

I Introduction: What are queer theologies?

Queer Christian theologies emerged in the 1990s and 2000s and are sometimes considered successors to the LGBT (lesbian, gay, bisexual and trans) theologies of the 1970s and beyond. The term 'queer' re-frames a word formerly used as a pejorative slur against gay people on the grounds that they were odd and abnormal. People who use the term queer positively today sometimes understand this as having 'turned' the insult, reclaiming it from their abusers, and see their 'oddness' and difference from 'mainstream' sexual and gender identities as a conscious refusal of them.[1]

Like LGBT theologies, queer theologies are often keen to disrupt the assumption that only heterosexual lives are licit, legitimate sites of grace, blessing and divine revelation. But queer theologies do not limit themselves to considerations of sexuality. Queer theologies usually involve a thoroughgoing disruption of norms of all kinds, asking questions about power, language, and the limits of identity. Queer acts as a noun, adjective or verb. As a noun, it refers to methods and approaches that question and subvert accepted norms and ideologies. As an adjective, it can refer to people, texts or other phenomena engaged in this broad project. As a verb, it has a variety of uses – but 'to queer' a tradition might, for example, mean asking what subversive or resisting voices have been latent, and perhaps suppressed, within it. Queering often entails asking questions about how some – and only some – identities have come to be understood as normal, healthy and desirable, and what kinds of power and ideology are hidden in the mechanisms through which widely-accepted understandings of normality have come into being.

Queer is sometimes used as shorthand for a range of identities and political positions: lesbian, gay, bisexual, trans, intersex, asexual, non-binary and more. However, many commentators resist the idea that queer can be used as an umbrella term to 'encompass' these identities. In fact, some are suspicious that to use queer in this way actually risks glossing over differences and tensions between these groups, erasing people who were already marginalized. They point out that non-heterosexuality in itself does not disturb the social systems that assume everyone is clearly and unambiguous male or female and that gender expression should map onto physical sex only in certain ways. Among queer critical theorists in particular, queer is more likely to be understood as a *disruption* of identity categories than an identity in its own right. So queer does not entail the replacement of one system by another better one, but rather a suspicion of systems and meta-narratives per se.[2]

Queer theologies more specifically might be understood as existing in two broad streams. The first, the queer-liberationist stream, focuses on the 'normality' and non-pathology of queer lives. It has a particular emphasis on reframing accounts of sex, gender and sexuality, and reclaiming the Christian tradition as healthy rather than hostile for LGBT and queer people. Queer theologians in this stream have been among those campaigning for the recognition of same-sex marriages, and for the acceptance of openly LGBT people as Christian clergy. Queer-liberationist theologians are likely to reclaim or rehabilitate biblical texts used to oppress non-heterosexual people. They argue that LGBT identities are just as natural and healthy as heterosexual ones. The second stream is less reparative, and is influenced more by queer critical theory than by liberation theologies. Queer theologians in this stream are likely to be less invested in apologetics and more invested in subversion and resistance. They are circumspect about the goods of queer 'inclusion' in institutions such as marriage and church leadership, pointing instead to the damage that traditional understandings of marriage and family may cause, and suggesting that queer people of faith should resist them, and church authority, still further. They are more suspicious of terms such as 'healthy' and 'natural', and are likely to hold – influenced by queer critical theorists such as Judith Butler, Michel Foucault and Lee Edelman – that understandings of health and nature are socially-constructed, not neutral or unchanging, and certainly not unambiguously good.

II Querying translation and interpretation

Theologians working in the queer-liberationist stream argue that Christianity itself is not inherently antithetical to LGBT and other queer lives. Rather, they suggest, homophobia, sexism and cisgenderism (prejudice against people who have transitioned gender or who understand themselves as neither masculine nor feminine) are distortions of the real message of Christianity, which is about love, justice and inclusion. Some theologians in this stream have embarked on reclamations of the tradition, trying to uncover 'proto-queer' texts, figures and traditions in the bible and in Christian history. For example, some queer Christians have suggested that biblical figures like David and Jonathan, Naomi and Ruth, and the eunuchs, might be understood as forerunners to today's queer people. These interpreters do not necessarily claim that David and Jonathan or Naomi and Ruth were gay or lesbian as we would understand those terms today (though some readers do make such claims): they might rather, however, hold that these figures are examples whose strong love for people of the same sex gives a model for other same-sex friendships and relationships.

The eunuch figures have been particularly important for trans, intersex, bisexual, lesbian and gay readers, because they seem to be examples of people who stand outside their society's typical structures of sex and gender and yet are not condemned for it (and are, in fact, sometimes considered particularly blessed: Isaiah 56 makes reference to eunuchs who will be given 'riches greater than sons and daughters', and an 'everlasting name which will not be cut off'). In Matthew 19, a passage containing Jesus' teaching on marriage and divorce, Jesus remarks that there are three kinds of eunuchs: those born that way, those made that way by others, and those who have made themselves eunuchs for the sake of the kingdom. Historically, 'eunuchs' was often understood metaphorically here, with 'eunuchs for the sake of the kingdom' being those who had elected not to marry or have their own families so that they could give greater service to the community: avowed celibates, for example. In recent decades, however, some scholars have suggested that 'eunuchs from birth' might be understood as being intersex people (those with congenital physical variations of sex), 'those made eunuchs by others' might be trans people (especially those who have had some kind of medical intervention to alter their bodies), and 'eunuchs for the sake of the kingdom' might be those who electively stand outside expected sex-gender norms in other ways. Nancy Wilson of the Metropolitan Community Church (an explicitly LGBT-inclusive denomination) goes so far as to say that if queer people are unable to see themselves represented among figures in the Bible, then it cannot be understood as their book.[3]

Several texts in the Bible have been used for many decades to demonstrate the illegitimacy of non-heterosexual sexual activity and, in some cases, orientation. They are sometimes collectively termed 'clobber texts' or 'texts of terror' (a phrase also used to refer to sexist, anti-female texts). Queer biblical interpreters have a range of approaches to texts of this kind. Some hold simply that these passages, particularly those in the Hebrew Bible, originated in a very different time and culture and are not binding on Christians today. They may point to other texts, on issues such as diet, dress and the keeping of slaves, which most Christians have come to understand as time- and culture-bound, and suggest that verses on same-sex activity should be regarded likewise. Others hold that, whilst the Bible still remains a prime authority and Christians today are not at liberty to dismiss portions of it, it is possible that the Bible requires reinterpretation in light of contemporary scholarship.

Some interpreters, for example, argue that terms translated 'homosexuals' in modern English Bibles are obscure, and might legitimately be translated otherwise. Scholars including Mark D. Jordan and Dale B. Martin have noted that biblical translation is always an interpretative process: translators never come to texts neutrally, but always already with assumptions and biases.[4] Translators who already expect the Bible to condemn homosexuality may be more likely to translate an obscure term in a list of sins as 'homosexuals': but at other times, when other issues provoked more anxiety than same-sex relationships do today, the same term may have been translated in quite other ways (as we can see if we look at older English translations). Even interpretation of translations can be freighted: Jordan and others note that the 'sin of Sodom' condemned on several occasions across the Bible is often assumed to be male-male sexual activity, or anal intercourse more specifically. However, holds Jordan, it was not until the medieval era that 'sodomy' was commonly understood in this way. Indeed, there is at least an ambiguity in what exactly is being condemned: is the problem that the men of Sodom had sex with other *men*, or was the problem that they were *angels* and therefore not licit sexual partners for humans? Jude 7, which condemns the people of Sodom and Gomorrah for their sexual immorality, does so on the grounds of their pursuit of 'other flesh' – which could, suggest some interpreters, refer to angels. Or, as many contemporary queer readers have come to believe, is the problem less the gender of those concerned, but the voracious violence, greed and inhospitality exhibited by the people of Sodom? After all, Ezekiel 16.49 says, 'This was the guilt of your sister Sodom: she and her daughters had pride, excess of food, and prosperous ease, but did not aid the poor and needy'.

These kinds of reframings of the Bible often have in common their desire to reclaim it as positive and liberating for queer people. However, such attempts may seem futile given that there are still plenty of Christians and others unpersuaded by such readings who see in the Bible clear condemnations of same-sex activity. For this reason, suggests Mary Ann Tolbert (2000), the Bible is likely to remain dangerous for queer people despite queer interpreters' best efforts to the contrary.[6]

III Querying decency, marginality and power in theological discourses

Queer theologians have also attempted to re-read and re-frame aspects of historical, moral, pastoral, doctrinal, systematic and constructive Christian theology in light of the concerns that queer theory highlights. One of the most influential queer theologians is Marcella Althaus-Reid, an Argentinian theologian whose work was curtailed by her early death in

2009. Althaus-Reid devised what she called an 'indecent' theology, which refused to separate off theology from the real circumstances of people's lives, including those whose sexual identities and practices would likely be condemned by mainstream Christianity. Althaus-Reid held that Christianity (particularly the Roman Catholicism of Latin America, influenced by alliances with colonial and capitalist powers) had been invested in maintaining 'decent' ideals unattainable and deeply damaging for ordinary people. Althaus-Reid devised a compelling account of what she called the Queer God: a God in exile, of the streets, of sex workers and drag queens, who continued to dwell with those at the margins rather than moving toward the privileged 'centre'. She held that theologians should embrace 'indecency', and reject the idea that salvation is something to be doled out in limited portions by those in positions of power. The tight control of sexual behaviour and reproduction wielded by the Church in Latin America was, she argued, less about protecting the good of the people and more about siding with political authorities to keep workers docile. Althaus-Reid believed Christianity had attempted to corral and domesticate God rather than recognizing God's profound otherness and inability to be possessed or controlled. She held that it was vital to resist heteronormativity (the idea that only heterosexuality is legitimate or desirable) and to speak the truth that the really outrageous thing was not sexual 'deviance' but the exclusion of such 'deviants' by religious and other authorities. Theology must, she insisted, learn to live with uncertainty and fluidity, and get beyond its obsession with boundaries and demarcating who was in and who was out. God, she said, is a stranger, living in diaspora: this is where Christians should also dwell. This will mean theologians must come to interrogate their own sexual, political and economic lives, rather than hiving these off from what happens in church: in short, for Althaus-Reid, 'God cannot be Queered unless theologians have the courage to come out from their [...] closets'.[7]

Some notable queer theologians active today, including Elizabeth Stuart, Gerard Loughlin, Robert E. Shore-Goss, and Mark D. Jordan,[8] knew and worked with Althaus-Reid. There is also a generation of younger and emerging scholars who have continued to be influenced by her work and to develop it in new directions. Some scholars (including Jay Emerson Johnson and Patrick S. Cheng) have been particularly invested in exploring queer theologies' outworkings within ecclesiastical structures, whilst others have explored the interactions between queer theology and questions of ethnicity, race, class, disability, climate change, and nationality, as well as re-reading and re-examining well-established theological approaches such as virtue ethics through a queer lens.[9] In all these cases, these scholars continue the project of interrogating how power rises up in multiple contexts, and how far the church's own sometime alliances with social and political authorities, and its own perpetuations of conservative norms of family, sexuality and relationship undermine its capacity to speak prophetically into situations of injustice.

IV Querying the historical Christian tradition

A common feature of queer theologies, particularly those more influenced by queer critical theory, is their rejection of binary distinctions – notably male and female, but also others such as human and divine. For this reason, theologians invested in 'uncovering' queerness right back through the historical Christian tradition have sometimes suggested that Christ himself, in his holding-together of humanity and divinity in one body, might be understood as profoundly queer. The scholar of patristics (early Christian theology) Virginia Burrus makes just this kind of claim when she says that the Chalcedonian creed (the affirmation that Christ held together two natures in one person) 'demands a new math, a calculus that exceeds the logic of addition and subtraction, of fractions and wholes' and thus goes 'beyond the categories'.[10] Tricia Sheffield agrees that the Christ imagined at Chalcedon is not either-or, but both-and: in this sense, he is queer, resisting binaries and divisions, holding together uncertainty, therefore paving the way for other 'ambiguous' identities in those who make up the Body of Christ, the Church. To say 'Christ is queer' is, then, not a claim about Jesus' sexual orientation or gender identity – though some readers have more explicitly wanted to disrupt the assumption that Jesus was necessarily heterosexual – but rather a claim about his disruption of expected norms, and solidarity with all queer people. In this way, Christ's queerness is read in and through the various ways he resists and subverts norms of power and control. To claim Christianity as queer is to ask how Christianity might help to uncover and bring to light hidden structures of power, oppression and control, including those within its own tradition.

In terms of classical doctrines of Christian theology, queer theology has been particularly influential in the areas of Christology (teachings about the person and work of Jesus), the doctrine of God (including Trinitarian theologies), ecclesiology (teachings about the Church), and eschatology (teachings about the 'last things', usually understood as including matters concerning death, judgement, the afterlife and the 'end times').

Since the 1960s, influenced in particular by the work of the German theologian Jürgen Moltmann, the Church has seen a revival of interest in eschatology. In Moltmann's own account, eschatology concerns not just the end of the world, or what might happen after death, but what goes on here and now. The work of Jesus and the Spirit is such that the 'new creation' has already begun to be brought into existence. Living lives marked by justice and inclusion might be understood as helping to live this new world into being. This kind of account underlies much queer-liberationist theology. However, queer-critical theologies have a more freighted relationship with doctrines of eschatology. Classically, eschatology is marked by hope for the future, for a time beyond death when the present things will have passed away. But some critical theorists, including Lee Edelman, are suspicious that investing too much in the future tends to have negative consequences for life here and now. In particular, future-oriented theologies often appeal to the need to make things better for the sake of children and other 'innocents'. However, such appeals tend to be socially-conservative and tend to sacrifice the goods of those alive now to the goods of putative future people.[12]

Althaus-Reid formulates an account of a queer God in solidarity with those marginalized for reasons including their sex, sexuality, gender, ethnicity, class, and economic status. Since her death, other theologians have developed the project of queer theology to interrogate the doctrine of God still further. Linn Marie Tonstad, for instance, persuasively argues that many classic theologians of the mainstream Christian tradition have been distinctly untroubled by the assumption that order, procession, hierarchy, sacrifice, death and alienation are built into the relationships in the Godhead. Attempts to find warrant for gender difference in God (like identifying the Spirit with the biblical figure of Lady Wisdom) actually, suspects Tonstad, just end up solidifying the sexed and gendered nature of divine hierarchy. Appeals to human sexed and gendered difference are often made to rest on accounts of divine difference via the Trinity; however much people might appeal to the Trinity to disrupt sexist and patriarchal accounts, suggests Tonstad, the doctrine of God itself is too bound-up with its sexist and patriarchal history to be of much use here.[13] This is just one example of queer theology's challenge to mainstream theological accounts of power and knowledge, highlighting that how we arrive at our understanding is never neutral but always impacted by our social, political and cultural circumstances – and emphasizing, too, the ways in which even challenges to power from within 'alternative' theologies can perpetuate their own problematic neo-orthodoxies which themselves require interrogation and critique.

V Recent developments in queer theology

Additional significant recent works in queer theology include Kent Brintnall, Joseph Marchal and Stephen D. Moore's 2018 collection *Sexual Disorientations*, which re-examines the theological and biblical traditions in conversation with queer anti-futurity, re-reading central themes such as eschatology, profiling the work of emerging queer scholars who draw on feminist, crip and critical race theory, including Brandy Daniels, Karen Bray and Jacqueline Hidalgo; Kathleen Talvacchia, Michael Pettinger and Mark Larrimore's edited volume *Queer Christianities*, critically reframing traditions of celibacy, marriage and 'excessive' sexuality from across the tradition; Pamela Lightsey's *Womanist Queer Theology* which sheds queer theological light on the politics of the Black Lives Matter movement; Andy Buechel's *That We Might Become God* which re-reads sacramental theology and traditions of theosis/divinization in conversation with queer concerns; and Robert Shore-Goss et al.'s anthology *Queering Christianity*, which takes a pastoral theological approach and focuses in on questions live in church life such as the queer significance of baptism, Eucharist and ecumenism. In my own work I show that institutions including marriage, parenting and family need not be understood as antithetical to queer concerns, nor that queer reframings of them constitute inherent breaks with the Christian tradition.[14]

Queer theology is no longer, then, if it ever was, primarily interested in sexuality and gender, but takes an intersectional approach which also requires interrogation of other contexts and identities such as ethnicity, disability, class and social location. In this way it has the potential to encourage reflection on faith communities and their activities in a kaleidoscopic perspective deeply committed to the pursuit of justice. Some of these more recent works respond directly to criticisms levelled at earlier queer theologies that they were too centred on white and male experience and took too little account of how these vectors of privilege had been concealed within 'liberalizing' theologies as well as more obviously conservative mainstream ones. It remains a conundrum within queer theology, as in queer theory more broadly, that queer is simultaneously understood as a way both to reclaim and re-frame formerly-marginalized identity perspectives, and to challenge the whole notion of identity *per se*.

VI Conclusion

Queer theology remains a profoundly self-reflexive area and one which is becoming increasingly better at examining its own, sometimes hidden, hierarchies and orthodoxies, particularly as these pertain to institutional (whether ecclesiastical or academic) 'acceptability'. That queer theologies are being discussed in churches and universities at all is understood as deeply ambivalent, since this kind of mainstreaming might diminish its capacity for critique. Yet the diversification of voices and perspectives – especially, though not exclusively, in terms of sexuality and gender identity – that queer theology brings to these arenas also represents a welcome means of reinterpreting and renewing aspects of the tradition.

Notes

1. For an accessible graphic overview of some historical and theoretical context, see Meg-John Barker and Julia Scheele, *Queer: A Graphic History*, London: Icon, 2016.
2. See further discussion in Susannah Cornwall, *Controversies in Queer Theology*, London: SCM Press, 2011; see also e.g. Judith Butler, *Gender Trouble: Feminism and the Subversion of Identity*, London: Routledge, 1990; Michel Foucault, T*he History of Sexuality: Volume 1: An Introduction*, London: Penguin, 1990; David Halperin, *Saint Foucault: Towards a Gay Hagiography*, Oxford: Oxford University Press, 1995.
3. Nancy Wilson, *Our Tribe: Queer Folks, God, Jesus, and the Bible*, San Francisco: HarperSanFrancisco, 1995, p. 164. For additional work on the significance of eunuchs see e.g. Mathew Kuefler, *The Manly Eunuch: Masculinity, Gender Ambiguity, and Christian Ideology in Late Antiquity*, Chicago: University of Chicago Press, 2001; Megan DeFranza, *Sex Difference in Christian Theology: Male, Female and Intersex in the Image of God*, Grand Rapids: Eerdmans, 2015; Virginia Mollenkott, *Omnigender: A Trans-Religious Approach*, Cleveland: Pilgrim Press, 2007.
4. Mark D. Jordan, *The Invention of Sodomy in Christian Theology*, Chicago: University of Chicago Press, 1997; Dale B. Martin, *Sex and the Single Savior: Gender and Sexuality in Biblical Interpretation*, Louisville: Westminster John Knox Press, 2006.
5. For additional useful queer critical engagements with the Bible see e.g. Deryn Guest, Robert Goss, Mona West and Thomas Bohache (eds.), *The Queer Bible Commentary*,

London: SCM Press, 2006; Ken Stone (ed.), *Queer Commentary and the Hebrew Bible*, Sheffield: Sheffield Academic Press, 2001; Teresa Hornsby and Ken Stone (eds.), *Bible Trouble: Queer Reading at the Boundaries of Biblical Scholarship*, Atlanta: Society for Biblical Literature, 2011.

6. Mary Ann Tolbert, 'Foreword: What Word Shall We Take Back?', in Robert Goss and Mona West (eds.), *Take Back the Word*, Cleveland: Pilgrim Press, 2000, pp. vii–xii.

7. Marcella Althaus-Reid, *Indecent Theology*, London: Routledge, 2000, p. 88.

8. For key texts see e.g. Elizabeth Stuart, *Gay and Lesbian Theologies: Repetitions with Critical Difference*, Aldershot: Ashgate, 2003; Gerard Loughlin (ed.), Queer Theology: Rethinking the Western Body, Oxford: Blackwell, 2007.

9. See e.g. Patrick S. Cheng, *Radical Love: An Introduction to Queer Theology*, New York: Seabury, 2011; Patrick S. Cheng, *Rainbow Theology: Bridging Race, Sexuality, and Spirit*, New York: Seabury, 2013; Jay Emerson Johnson, *Peculiar Faith: Queer Theology for Christian Witness*, New York: Seabury, 2014; Karen Bray, 'The Monstrosity of the Multitude: Unredeeming Radical Theology', *Palgrave Communications*, 1 (2015), doi:10.1057/palcomms.2015.30; see also essays in Kent Brintnall, Joseph Marchal and Stephen D. Moore (eds.), *Sexual Disorientations: Queer Temporalities, Affects, Theologies*, New York: Fordham University Press, 2018.

10. Virginia Burrus, 'Radical Orthodoxy and the Heresiological Habit: Engaging Graham Ward's Christology', in Rosemary Radford Ruether and Marion Grau (eds.), *Interpreting the Postmodern: Responses to 'Radical Orthodoxy'*, New York: T&T Clark, 2006, p. 40.

11. Tricia Sheffield, 'Performing Jesus: A Queer Counternarrative of Embodied Transgression', *Theology and Sexuality*, 14 (2008), 243.

12. Lee Edelman, *No Future: Queer Theory and the Death Drive*, Durham: Duke University Press, 2004.

13. Linn Marie Tonstad, *God and Difference: The Trinity, Sexuality, and the Transformation of Finitude*, London: Routledge, 2015.

14. Kathleen Talvacchia, Michael Pettinger and Mark Larrimore (eds.), *Queer Christianities: Lived Religion in Transgressive Forms*, New York: New York University Press, 2015; Pamela Lightsey, *Our Lives Matter: A Womanist Queer Theology*, Eugene: Wipf and Stock, 2015; Andy Buechel, *That We Might Become God: The Queerness of Creedal Christianity*, Eugene: Cascade, 2015; Robert Shore-Goss, Thomas Bohache, Patrick S. Cheng and Mona West (eds.), *Queering Christianity: Finding a Place at the Table for LGBTQI Christians*, Santa Barbara: Praeger, 2013; Susannah Cornwall, *Un/familiar Theology: Reconceiving Sex, Reproduction and Generativity*, London: Bloomsbury, 2017.

Part Two: Experiences

Queer is God

MURPH MURPHY

This text explores the experience of Murph, a non-binary queer identified white person, raised in a conservative Catholic community in the United States of America. They came to embrace their queerness through community, movement, and dancing. Murph explains the way they feel and act queer as a divine form of resistance, creation, and expression of life.

I danced my way to home to myself, I danced myself queer. Before I found dancing, I hated my body, I hated being in my body. I was a stranger to myself, to my soul, to my truth. I grew up in an institutional church that culturally and religiously rejected bodies, especially female, black, brown, disabled, trans and queer bodies. As a small child, I did what felt right to me. I found life dressing like the boys while playing street hockey, dancing, playing football, building things, climbing trees, skinning my knees, playing cars and superheroes. I lived outside of societal norms; I lived queerly. Around the age of ten, my body began to feel more public, more policed; this was the beginning of a process of disembodiment. On a public level, my queerness was taken hostage by the empires of patriarchy, institutional church and capitalism.

I felt like a guest in my young female body and I did everything I could to survive adolescence. I had to play the game of modest young women that my family, community and society expected me to play. I needed to survive. So, I dressed in clothes that I hated, I tamed my wild curly hair and tamed my wild spirit. I learned that being female bodied meant I could not question the status quo including prescribed gender roles. I was forced to live a life that felt inherently wrong and violent in my skin.

Murph Murphy

This false façade led me into several years of depression, social anxiety, eating disorders, dysmorphia, shame and several decades of isolation. This inauthentic version of me led me to believe my life was over before it began. Conforming to the system killed my personhood, killed my spirit, killed my unique divinity. I continue to battle against these deadly symptoms of institution. The weeds and seeds of oppressive systemic homophobia and sexism live deep within my bones and I must continually tend to the invasions as they arise.

    I danced my way to home to myself, I danced myself queer. Life is full of emotional, spiritual, mental and eventually physical sicknesses, deaths and resurrections. I lived as a cis-white female for the first 24 years of my life. I grew up in the epicentre of Catholic hetero-patriarchy. I belong to a white middle- to lower-class Irish Catholic family in the United States. I felt that my only option was to attend school, get a well-paying job, get married to a man and have children. In my limited understanding of self and possibility, this predetermined lifestyle was the only way I could get through life. Life was mine to survive, it was mine to get through

    It was in my early formation that I unknowingly digested rhetoric that LGBTQ+ folx were sinners, dirty, meant to burn in hell. Being gay or lesbian was one of my greatest fears. I didn't know the difference between sexuality and gender, and I didn't want to know. I didn't want to talk about it. I didn't want to have ownership of it because I didn't want to be abnormal and outcast. I feared coming out as my true self. I feared the death of my false identity and communities that felt both stifling and safe. I avoided knowing myself until I could no longer bear the weight of avoidance.

    It wasn't until I moved far away from my birth place that I understood embodied sexuality and gender. And I didn't really understand it as much as feel it. I first listened to other people's experiences of queerness and found deep resonance. I found people who allowed me the grace and time to move into my authentic expression of self and unique queerness without putting me in a box. I also encountered many people who immediately hated me simply because they fear change, difference and creativity. They fear that my being alive is a threat to their false sense of safety and power. I am a gender non-binary person with a female body who is attracted to women and other female bodied persons. And I wear that identity loudly, proudly, and fluidly.

Queer is God

I really began to excavate my queerness in my mid-to-late-twenties while living in a new culture in Nicaragua. Being raised Catholic, my upbringing entombed me in a deep sense of shame, fear, guilt and judgement. At this point in my life, I still felt like a foreigner in my own body. I felt shame and guilt for having a female body, sexuality and fluid gender. During these years, I underwent so many personal deaths and liberating resurrections regarding identity.

I came home to myself while living in community. I unpacked and worked against personal and global forms of oppression and marginalization while celebrating and sharing food, stories, laments and joys. Dancing in clubs, in groups, in classes, in my home, in the street taught me to feel my body, move creatively and express my spirit in spite of the pressures to stay small, quiet and in line. It wasn't until I flew from my comfort zones and said yes to dance in community, learn rhythm, learn to move individually and collectively that I gained the courage to be who I am with pride. Dancing became a platform which I used to own my personhood.

When listening to my body while moving in the world, creativity flows out of my being. In these moments, it becomes impossible to not let myself been seen and known, first by myself and then by others. Whether it's dancing, writing, sharing stories, painting, singing, laughing – there is a vulnerability and knowing that stems from your soul. It was through this continuous exposure to vulnerable movement in safe community that I began to live into and embody my queer identity. Without having language or knowledge, the way I dressed, carried myself and related to all beings began to change. I lived once more as I did as a child – outside of binary or social laws that dictated who I was supposed to be. I am a born-again queer who was redeemed by divine creativity and movement.

Queer feels most courageous and alive when used as a verb. It is a reclaimed term that weaves in, out and beyond limitations. Queer expands and erases borders that do not serve us. Therefore, queer cannot be properly defined by a dictionary. Each lived experience of queerness, which is not limited to describing one's gender or sexuality, is unique and expansive. Queer is divine creation that will not be tamed or used against anyone. Just as God is an action word, just as God creates, lives, dies, and is reborn within all life – so is queerness. Queer is God.

It wasn't until I learned to express my being through movement and connection that I too began to understand that I am sacred. All queer bodies are God and divine. And all bodies are queer. All bodies, minds and souls are capable of loving self and all life beyond laws, religions, walls, languages, politics, war and hatred. Let us all dance, sing, laugh, create and love our way home to ourselves, to the divine, to radical queerness.

The Will of God

FR. PAUL UCHECHUKWU

A life story about negotiating religious and sexual identity in an African Context. This also includes some of the challenges faced as well as inspirations and hopes that have helped along the journey towards integration.

After having two boys, my parents earnestly prayed for a girl. When my mum became pregnant with me, my parents were convinced I was going to be a girl. Even though I was born a boy, they accepted me gladly and said God must have wanted me that way, hence my name, *Uchechukwu*, meaning 'the will of God.'

I first heard the word 'homosexual' when I was eleven years old while in boarding school. I was lying down beside a close friend of mine, and we were talking and laughing. Another student passed by and said, 'why are you guys all cuddled up like this, are you homosexuals?' I asked my friend what that word meant and when he told me, I immediately left him and scurried back to my bunk. I was terrified because I had this sexual attraction toward him which I could not explain. It also seemed 'wrong' to me coming from a strong Catholic family where I was baptized as an infant, received my first Communion at the age of ten and was confirmed three years later. In my family, sexuality and sex were taboo topics, and my parents always emphasized that we were never to have sex until marriage.

Throughout high school and university, I was aware of an attraction to the same sex, but it was an awareness that came and went quickly. Sometimes, when the feelings were overwhelming, I would pray to God to take them away. No one talked about 'these things', and the internet wasn't easily accessible then. While in university, I was still a 'virgin' in the sense that I had never been involved sexually with anyone. I was caught up with studies and very active in the Catholic Charismatic movement. I eventually talked to a priest about my same-sex feelings, and he told me that they were satanic and that if I ever gave in to them, I would find myself being a paedophile. As penance, he asked me to do the Stations of the Cross. Being a perfectionist, I did them three times, one of them on my knees. What the priest said to me on that day stuck in my mind, and it took a while before I was healed from it. I graduated *summa cum laude* with a bachelor in Economics and decided to enter the seminary in order to be a priest, a calling I felt I had from childhood.

I joined a Missionary Order, and my formators (mostly European) helped me to come to a place of naming and accepting my sexuality by suggesting some books to help me. Theologian James Alison, whose emails, phone calls, and friendship were sources of encouragement for me, sent me many of these books which helped me in my journey towards psycho-sexual integration. The ones that impacted me most include: *Faith Beyond Resentment* by James Alison,[1] *Embracing The Exile* by John Fortunato,[2] *Taking A Chance On God* by John McNeill[3] and *What The Bible Really Says About Homosexuality* by Daniel Helminiak.[4] The greatest challenge was that even though my seminary studies were outside my home country, I had yet to see something written about gay matters by an African. Later on, when I met Jide Macaulay, a very courageous British-Nigerian theologian, writer, and poet, I knew that I was not alone.[5]

It was, however, during a period of pastoral work that I came to a place of radical acceptance of who I was as a gay man. I was still a bit conflicted about my sexuality. I was working in a hospital, and during my lunch break, I snuck away to the chapel for a few minutes of prayer, and I fell asleep. I had a dream in which a beautiful lady who seemed to come from the tabernacle came towards where I was sitting in the chapel and hugged me while saying, 'It's okay, you're okay.' When I woke up, even though I was somewhat terrified, I wept uncontrollably, after which I felt a deep peace within me that I hadn't felt before. I never doubted myself again after that day. During my theological studies, I focused on Scriptures and graduated with a first class degree. By this time, I had managed to integrate my sexuality with my identity as a whole. I focused on my vocation to the priesthood, and I was out to some close friends.

The Will of God

While working as a missionary priest in 2014, I heard that a law had been passed by the Nigerian government criminalizing relationships between gay persons, with prison sentences of up to fourteen years. I was disappointed that some bishops approved of this law which led to increased victimization and attacks of LGBTQ persons and suspected LGBTQ persons. I wrote an article condemning this law, and it drew a lot of criticism from some of my African confrères. Years later, while working in the seminary back home, I was shocked at how homophobic people were. One of our priests preached a sermon in which he abused and mocked LGBT persons. There was also another case of a man who was beaten to death close to our seminary because he was gay. The seminarians supported his being beaten to death.

I tried to 'educate' them on the fact that gay persons were also human beings through classes and some educational movies. One of the students who confessed his homophobia to me, and another priest, who confessed to being allergic to gay persons, filed a report to my superiors accusing me of being 'too friendly' with the students and also of trying to 'promote homosexuality'. I was asked to leave the seminary and sent to work in another diocese outside the country. The bishop there, on hearing about my sexual orientation, decided he didn't want to employ a priest who was gay because of past cases of the abuse of children by priests. I was asked to leave the diocese, and this became the lowest point of my life. I had not broken my vows or done anything wrong. The thought of being compared to a paedophile made me angry and sick to my stomach. I simply suffered because of stereotypes and the ignorance concerning gay persons.

I suffered a severe depression and took some time out to go to Europe for counselling, rest and self-care. It was a healing experience: when I attended a retreat for LGBTQI persons, the retreatants came around me and placed their hands on my shoulders. When they prayed with me, I felt the same way I had felt many years before in that chapel. I felt that I belonged, that I mattered and that hate was not going to take away the love which God has placed in my heart. I felt peaceful.

I returned renewed from my mini-sabbatical. I also re-discovered contemplative spirituality through the writings of the Franciscan priest, Richard Rohr, which has been very helpful to me. It's clear to me now that I may never work at home, in my country, but I'm quite happy and content where I am. I feel that despite what I've been through, my sexuality has made me more compassionate as a priest. A lot of homophobia comes from ignorance and while I now know that the burden of informing and changing people's mindset doesn't rest on my shoulders, in my own small way, I still try. Recently, a mother brought her young son to me for counselling because she thought him possessed by the devil. He had stopped coming to church, and when I asked him about it, he said he thought he was an abomination to God because he was gay. I opened my Bible and read these words to him from Wisdom 11:24: 'You hate none of the things you have made, for you would not have made anything you hated.' A former student whom I taught in seminary wrote and thanked me for what I shared with them during my time in the seminary. He's now happy as a gay man and quite fulfilled with his life. I know we still have a long way to go towards the full acceptance of LGBTQI persons in Church and society, but I'm happy that attitudes are changing, albeit gradually. I find inspiration from people like Fr. James Martin SJ, an American Jesuit priest who emphasizes building bridges between the Church and LGBTQI persons. I see a lot of hope in many LGBTQI persons who continue to love and serve the Church despite the hate they often receive. But most of all, I find peace within my heart where I hear the Spirit whisper to me, 'You are not a disorder, you are Uchechukwu, the will of God'.

Notes

1. James Alison, *Faith Beyond Resentment*, New York: The Crossroad Publishing Company, 2001.
2. John Fortunato, *Embracing the Exile: Healing Journeys of Gay Christians*, San Francisco: Harper San Francisco, 1984.
3. John J. McNeill, *Taking a Chance on God*, Boston: Beacon Press, 1988, 1996.
4. Daniel Helminiak, *What the Bible Really Says About Homosexuality*, New Mexico: Alamo Square Press, 2000.
5. Jide Macaulay is the founding pastor of the House of Rainbow Fellowship. He is British-Nigerian, born in London, a Christian minister since 1998 and focuses his ministry on inclusion and reconciliation of sexuality, spirituality and human rights.

Letter from a Reluctant Indian

LUKAS AVENDAÑO

Here the story is told in the first person of the muxe condition, something more than a third gender, in the Zapotec cultural tradition of the southeast of Mexico. It is the narrative of a decolonial process of the affirmation of diverse subjectivities, where the gender, ethnicity, and politics of the emancipation of diasporic bodies intersect. Within this reflective testimony flows a spirituality of liberation, with powerful words and metaphors of being for and with other subjectivities in resistance, rebellion, and hope.

I Taking a look at *muxe*idad

The reflections that follow give an account of the influence that liberation theology had on me, promoted by Bishop Don Arturo Lona, in the Diocese of Tehuantepec, when I was a young student and participated in the base communities in the Zapotec context: There I learned to reconcile my *muxe* condition with a spirituality of life.

The quality of *muxe* in the context of the Isthmus of the Tehuantepec contrasts with being *muxe* outside the region. In the Isthmus, *muxe* is a distinctive cultural expression of the milenary culture *zaa* (Zapotec/binni zaa/zaa). Outside of the Isthmus, in the eyes of the other, I am *puto* (male whore)/gay or another similar designation.

Some local knowledge affirms that the *muxe* has existed or co-existed ancestrally in the Zaa culture. But when you ask, how long has *muxe* existed? Some will answer: 'Ever since Adam and Eve ate the Apple and were expelled from Paradise, the world was twisted.' Others will say that 'when Saint Vincente Ferrer (1350-1419), the Dominican patron saint of Juchitán, was going around the world with a bag full of *putos*, scattering them, the bag ripped, and from there they multiplied. Some more will answer: 'from who knows when.'

The first two ways of explaining the origin of *muxeity* place the existence of the *muxe* in a specific time. In the version of Eve and Adam, the *muxe* has existed since the world was twisted: *muxe* exists from the beginning; but the expression 'twisted' makes them seem imperfect, touched by sin, disapproved of by God as a consequence of disobedience! In the second form, the emergence in the sixteenth century is narrated through Saint Vincent Ferrer. Both expressions, appeal to Christian stories, which by default detracts from the validity of the premise that *muxeity* is a legitimately Zaa expression, since it endows it with a Western temporality, putting it into a context that does not exist in the Zaa worldview. However, in the third expression, 'from who knows when', it is possible that the 'who' is anyone who can report the existence of *muxeity* from times prior to peninsular contact. And to understand this difference I propose two hypotheses.

First hypothesis: 'Grace.' In the Zapotec communities or with Zaa descent communities, it is often said "There's no grace with you!", as a form of disapproval. Or also, "They sure have grace!", as approval, recognizing some ability in the person for aesthetic expressions such as creating floral ornaments, dancing, designing textiles, talking, walking, putting on makeup, telling jokes with humour, etc. This grace accompanies the *muxe* and defines them as being of grace, which includes orality: anecdotes, jokes, stories, or the simple act of speaking that is done with grace. They are not grace! But it is the grace that exists in them.

Second hypothesis: 'Grace = *Guenda*'. Among the speakers of didxazaa (Zapotec) exists a Word that is substituted by the word in Castilian 'grace' and is '*guenda*', the 'being'. All things – also people – possess their *guenda*, even the words are now endowed with *guenda*. When children are a few days old, while they sleep they make faces or gestures that make them seem to laugh. Then, the inhabitants of the Santa Cruz Tagolaba neighbourhood, in Tehuantepec, ask adults not to look at them and cover the baby with a handkerchief "so that they do not steal its *guenda*' or angel, since what the newborn does at that time, expressed in gestures, is 'talk' with its *guenda*. Is it a translation of the Mesoamerican tonal and nagual?

If then *guenda* is being, it is also creative energy. And when it is associated with *muxeity*, we can say that a connection has been found that links the co-existence of *muxeity* with Zaa culture since pre-Columbian times. Thus, we have in the *guenda* the first vestiges of *muxe* existence in the Zaa culture, at least since the post-classical Zapotec period. While *guenda* helps us understand why it is that 'being *muxe*' is associated with grace, it is important to do a long-term exercise, following Fernand Braudel, when he says that what takes the longest to change in societies is 'mentalities', because they are crossed by the situation, the event, and the *longue durée*. I say then, that both *guenda* and grace at this moment find their explanation in the *longue durée*, although first was the event/ situation.

II *Muxeity* as a subversive practice

Muxe exists to the extent that it is a 'total social fact'. Therefore, it is not appropriate to speak of *muxe*, but of *muxeity*. It would be necessary to consider many other variables that not only concern the *muxe*, but also masculinities, femininity, and the rite of passage of 'deflowering', eroticism, and sensuality for life in the broadest sense. In the eyes of the dxu – others/ outsiders – the *muxe*s are a matriarchal, xoophilic, paedophilic, and barbaric society because they behead bulls, goats, pigs, chickens, celebrate and exhibit the blood of the tearing of the hymen of virgins, and clearly are also permissive and tolerant of homosexuals.

If *muxe* exists as a third gender, it exists within the sociocultural fabric of the collectivity. The collectivity is the one that states, makes visible, and names, giving real or symbolic existence. *Muxe*s contribute social, economic, or symbolic capital, which is re-capitalized to the extent that they are inserted in the cultural practices of that community, fulfilling the commitments, participating in internal dynamics. This 'third gender' is built only on the daily participation of all public and private spheres, which means being a community!

In the logic of capitalism no one has any other way of being but competing, comparing themselves. And since in capitalism, tradition is not a value to be exchanged or that generates money, neither is it a good of surplus value. Therefore, our traditions are outside competition because *muxe* will never say that they are the best prayer in the neighbourhood or that they adorn the saint or the virgin more beautifully for the fiesta. They only strive as an instinctive/empirical gesture through their character of *guenda*/grace. One quality of 'being *muxe*' is the vocation of service for the community. Is a *muxe* manifestation out of context really generating community and collectivity? Does it strengthen the social fabric on which it is inaugurated and configuted? Or is it a queer strategy to break into the hegemonic subjectivities of their respective contexts?

In the case of people with 'gift'/*guenda*, if they acted out using it with the desire of the claim, they could lose it: the *guenda* leaves you, the greater the desire to compete, the greater the uprooting of the 'gift'. The *muxe* does not move because he is the best, his *guenda* moves, as a grace with his desire to serve, to fulfil the commitment and the promise. Hence the spirit of detachment, of giving, of distributing their real or symbolic goods, of accumulating and then wasting, like the potlatch among the Wakiut. This manifestation of offering/offering oneself to help, to serve, is what gives the *muxe* a social recognition with respect and place in the social structure, because all this is inherent in his person and his condition. Because they have *guenda*/grace and not because they are the best.

III To conclude

Muxeity is a way of life circumscribed to a geographical space in the region of the Isthmus of Tehuantepec, in the state of Oaxaca, which is latent in societies with Zapotec 'ethnic style'.

Muxeity, outside the Isthmus of Tehuantepec, is 'polygamy', 'incest', 'rape', an irrational condition, superstition, beliefs, frauds, idolatries, sodomy, and an abominable sin that inhabits with all the evil rancour a filthy homosexual body.

Muxeity is 'protagonized' by people who are born with 'penis and testicles', and who live their daily lives assuming cultural roles considered 'non-masculine trades, roles, aesthetics and/or tastes not of men'.

Muxeity is a poetics of life and a less orthodox subjectivity to experience bodies that contrast also with the scrupulous gaze of heteronormativity.

Muxeity is a rampant economy generating surpluses capable of being the providers of the family nucleus, generous with nieces and nephews and their parents, practiced from the guelaguetza (a form of neighbourhood community), the *guenda*liza, communal work, the everyday and more.

Muxeity is an aesthetic that is reflected in the forms and ways of decorating festive spaces.

Muxeity is a deliberate, open, and frank way of questioning and declaring false some patriarchal statement as 'criteria of truth'.

Muxeity is a zealous bastion of syncretic religiosity and of the nakedness of saints and virgins.

Muxeity is the hand on which fathers and mothers rely in their old age.

Muxeity is a way to begin to discover yourself in the exercise of sexuality without fear, without guilt, without regret, and without pre-conceived sins.

Muxeity is a way of contradicting Leviticus 20.13.

Muxeity is the rupture of the Judeo-Christian paradigm of sexuality, the private property of the body, the heteronormative family, and monogamy.

Muxeity is a possibility of falling in love and being happy, even if he only visits.

Muxeity is being finally self-sufficient and having a bed that is occasionally warmed by a casual lover.

Muxeity is to be the choreographer the quinceañera of women in the neighbourhood of the region.

Muxeity is to be trained as an alpha male, although the "silverback" is nail polish and chest hair is extensions or feathers on their head.

Muxeity is a Mesoamerican vessel that did not become a museum piece.

Muxeity is a codex saved from the eternal flames of hell.

Muxeity is a polysemic signifier.

Muxeity is an alphabet and *muxe* a phoneme.

Muxeity is the way of a collectivity's recognizing its own values, forms and rhythms.

Translated by Thia Cooper

Part Three: Theologies

Queering Jewish Theology in Parables

GWYNN KESSLER

This essay applies queer theories of gender fluidity and gender performativity to readings of rabbinic parables. Although parables in rabbinic literature have been explored for their theological insights, they have not been placed in conversation with understandings of gender that emerge from queer theory. This essay suggests that queer readings of parables offer a compelling counter-narrative to an always and singularly rigid, binary construction of gender in rabbinic sources. Rabbinic parables, which highlight gender fluidity, multiplicity, and instability, illuminate a queer theology at the heart of rabbinic understandings of gender, God, and Israel.

I Introduction

This essay reads rabbinic parables as texts saturated with theology and gender.[1] I explore how the intimate, immanent, engendered relationship(s) portrayed between Israel and God within rabbinic parables (*meshalim*) challenge a more common reading of rabbinic constructions of gender as best characterized by a rigid, stable male-female binary. I employ two aspects central to queer theory – gender instability and gender performativity – in order to illuminate a queer theology at the heart of rabbinic understandings of gender, God, and Israel.

At the outset, I want to take note of a serendipitous connection between parables and gender performativity. If gender is now, somewhat famously, not what one *is* but what one *does*, so too the parable. As A.J. Levine writes about parables,[2] 'We might be better off thinking less about what they "mean" and more about what they can "do": remind, provoke, refine, confront, disturb'.[3] So too, queer theory's investigations into gender are meant to provoke, confront, disturb, and yet ultimately refine and further our knowledge about gender. Throughout this essay, I focus not on what parables are and what they mean – especially in any singular way – but on what *meshalim do*. Put simply, what rabbinic parables do is offer countless compelling counter-narratives to an always and singularly rigid, binary construction of rabbinic gender.

The first section of this essay presents some aspects of Israel's gender fluidity, or instability, in rabbinic parables, and the second section explores how gender performativity provides an important, novel lens through which to examine parables. The final section shifts to a concern with God's gender in rabbinic parables, querying whether they may offer images of God that destabilize assumptions of exclusive maleness.

II Gender fluidity

Rabbinic parables foreground, even depend on, constructions of gender that are more fluid and unstable than rigid or fixed. For my purposes here, gender fluidity is defined as any movement among genders, encompassing 'gender-bending' as well as so-called 'gender reversals.' Such gender fluidity appears in rabbinic parables in two prominent ways. First, male figures, whether individual biblical figures or collective Israel, are compared or conflated with female figures. This likening, which assumes similarity, comparability, and fluidity between male and female genders, appears in multiple ways, for example, through applying a biblical verse about women to male characters and/or likening a male figure (e.g. Moses) to the female figure (wife of the king/God) within the parable. The second aspect of gender fluidity is that the gendered representations of Israel and other (male) figures populating rabbinic parables are not themselves stable or fixed. Some examples will help illustrate these points.

Genesis Rabbah 39.1 juxtaposes two scriptural verses, Genesis 12.1, which is God's address to Abraham (Avram) to leave his native land and his father's house, and Psalm 45.11, which urges a daughter to leave her people and her father's house for the king who desires her. The parable applies the verse in Psalm 45.11 that refers to a daughter to Abraham:

'*And God said to Avram, Get thee out of your country* (Gen 12.1). R. Yitzhak opened: *Hearken, O daughter, and see, and incline thine ear; forget also your own people, and your father's house* (Ps 45.11). R. Yitzhak said, 'This may be compared to a man who was passing from place to place and he saw a building aflame. He said, "You might say that this building has no one to look after it." The owner of the building looked out and said to him, "I am the building's owner." So too, Abraham our father, when he said, "You might say that this world has no one to look after it," the Holy Blessed One looked out and said, "I am the one who oversees all of the world." *And the king will desire your beauty* (Ps 45.12) – to make your beauty known in the world; *Because he is your lord and you should bow to him* (Ps 45.12). And God said to Avram, Get thee...'

I open with this text not so much to assert that Abraham is here made female, or that the text posits a clear, singular 'gender-reversal.' Rather, while the text first likens Abraham to a daughter, gendering him female through the application of Psalm 45 to him, the text also refers to him as 'Abraham our father'. Abraham's gender is thus depicted as fluid, defying and destabilizing a rigid male-female binary, as he embodies both a daughter whose beauty God desires and the patriarch of Israel.

Many rabbinic parables portray God and male biblical figures or God and Israel as husband and wife, building on spousal metaphors that are prominent in the Hebrew Bible. In the following parable, Moses is portrayed as the wife of God and Moses and God are imagined as the parents of Israel:

'A *mashal*: To what may this be compared? Moses is like a king's wife who was about to depart from the world. She said to him, "My lord the king, I charge you concerning my children." He said to her, "Do not command me concerning my children, command my children about Me!" So too, when Moses said before the Holy Blessed one, "Master of the Universe, since you are removing me from this world, make known to me what leaders you will make stand for Israel"' (*Ecclesiastes Rabbah* on 1.10).

Here Moses is likened to God's wife, and Israel's mother, who worries about Israel and their well-being after his pending death. God takes offense at Moses's questioning, responding that Moses does not command

God about God's own children, but commands God's children about God. In other words, a wife/mother does not rule over a husband/king, but supports him by instructing his children.

In another parable, Israel is imagined as, or plays, God's wife:

> '*And you shall write them upon the door posts of your house* (Deut 6.9). Precious are Israel, for Scripture has surrounded them with commandments: tefillin on their heads, tefillin on their arms, *mezuzot* on their doors, *tzitzit* on their garments [...]
> A parable of a king of flesh and blood who said to his wife, "bedeck yourself in all your finest jewellery in order that you be desirable to me." So too, the Holy Blessed One said to Israel, "Mark yourself with commandments in order that you will be desirable to me." And thus it says, *You are beautiful my darling, as Tirzah* (Song 6.4), i.e., you are beautiful when you are desirable to me' (*Sifre Deuteronomy* 36).

Here, the text portrays Israel as God's wife, dressed in her finest jewellery – the commandments of *tefillin*, *tzitzit*, and circumcision. These three *mitzvot*, so clearly gendered male insofar as according to halakhah (Jewish law) only men are obligated and permitted to perform them, are here performed by Israel imagined as God's *wife*. The parable thus simultaneously portrays Israel as female, insofar as they are God's wife, and male, insofar as they perform commandments that are constitutive of Israelite males.

The fluidity of Israel's gender in rabbinic parables is further exemplified when one incorporates *meshalim* that draw on familial relationships between God and Israel beyond husband and wife. This next parable first portrays Israel as God's son, and then as the female lover in the Song of Songs. The text states:

> 'This is likened to a king who had a son who went away to a far off country. He went after him and stood by him. The son went to another country, and the king again went after him and stood by him. So also, when Israel went down to Egypt, the Shekinah went down with them, as it is said, *I myself will go down with you to Egypt* (Gen 46.4). When they came up from Egypt, the Shekinah came up with them, as it is said, *And I myself will also bring you back* (Gen 46.4). When they went

into the sea, the Shekinah was with them, as it is said, *And the angel of God...journeyed* (Ex 14.19). When they went out into the wilderness, the Shekinah was with them, as it is said, *And the Lord went before them by day* (Ex 13.21) until they brought him with them to his holy Temple. *And so it says, Scarce had I passed them'* (Song 3.4).

At the start of this passage, God and Israel are likened to a father and a son. As a father follows his son, so God follows Israel – to God's very temple. Thus God, here as Shekinah, accompanies Israel to Egypt and back and to the sea and through the wilderness until, it seems, Israel delivers God to God's own temple. The last line of the text, however, shifts the representation of Israel from God's son to Israel as God's female lover with the quote from the female protagonist of the Song of Songs, which reads in full, 'Scarce had I passed them, when I found him whom my soul loves; I held him and would not let him go, until I had brought him into my mother's house, and into the chamber of her that conceived me' (Song 3.4). By the end of this passage, and I will return to this below, not only has Israel shifted from God's son to God's female lover, but God's temple is now reconfigured as Israel's *mother's* house.

Each of these parables demonstrate gender fluidity, a movement among genders, thus destabilizing rigid, binary constructions of gender. Abraham is portrayed as God's daughter, through the application of Psalm 45.12 to him, yet he is also presented as 'Abraham our Father'. Israel is portrayed as God's wife, though performing quintessentially male *mitzvot*. And Israel is portrayed as both God's son and God's female lover. Further, even though Moses performs the role of God's wife in the parable cited above, the audience comes to the text knowing Moses as male, and thus Moses is portrayed as always already performing maleness ('Moses our Rabbi'), and here simultaneously, performing femaleness (Moses as Mother/Wife).

III Gender performativity

One of the most exciting aspects of exploring rabbinic constructions of gender in *meshalim* specifically is that parables provide an intentionally discursive space where gender exceeds the boundaries of the body. There is no pretence that gender is confined to physical gender, or what is commonly referred to as 'biological sex'. Israel is no doubt understood as a collective entity comprised of men, but they are, often, simultaneously rendered female in relation to God.[4] In rabbinic parables, gender is not constituted by bodies, but by performative acts within particular relational matrices.

At the heart of rabbinic parables is a fluid construction of gender, with figures moving back and forth among genders, rather than an untraversable male-female binary. Parables depend not so much on the categories of male and female being 'reversed', as being mutually inhabited. If parables depended on a fixed male-female binary construction of gender, one that operated in terms of opposites rather than likenesses, or fixity instead of fluidity, *then they would fail* – they would be rendered unintelligible by an audience and rejected. Instead, rabbinic parables become powerful vehicles for theological exploration, for lending voice to the varied ways in which the rabbis of antiquity articulated the relationship between Israel and God.

There is some scholarly debate about whether *meshalim* equate the varied figures that appear in the two sections of typical rabbinic parables: the parable proper (*mashal*) and its application (*nimshal*). The question is usually posed when considering the relationship, be it conflation or comparison, between the 'king' in the parable proper and God in its application. But the question is at least implicitly posed for the figures Israel portrays or 'plays.' Is Israel equated, even conflated and collapsed with various figures to whom they are compared, or does Israel merely approximate them? Is Israel really God's wife, son, daughter, lover, etc.? Theories of performativity, which highlight *doing* as opposed to *being*, move us beyond such a scholarly impasse. We need not determine who Israel or God *is*, but instead we are invited to explore what God and Israel *do* – what roles they play, or more precisely which acts constitute them as Israel and God in relation with each other. From the vantage point of theories of performativity, which we may recall are shared by both parables and queer understandings of gender, the focus becomes how both God and Israel are constituted through performative acts within varied intimate relationships.

Judith Butler's productive theorizing of gender performativity has often been criticized based on a selective reading of her work. Much of the criticism arises from neglecting to take seriously the ever-present constraints Butler emphatically acknowledges that society, or language, imposes, which work to make a heterosexual, male-female gender binary system appear natural, even inevitable. In the final section of this essay, I consider potential constraints posed by parables, shifting my focus from Israel's gender(s) to that of God's gender. The rabbinic parables discussed thus far, though exhibiting gender fluidity on Israel's part, have remained consistent in portraying God as male (king, father, husband, etc.). God's presumptive maleness in *meshalim* does not mean theories of gender performativity are not applicable; maleness is as performative as other genders. The question explored in the following section takes God's gender performativity for granted, it merely takes up the challenge of the presumptive exclusiveness of God's maleness in rabbinic literature.

IV God's gender(s)
Almost fifty years have passed since feminist scholarship has unearthed traces of female images of God in the Hebrew Bible.[5] To my knowledge, little has been done on a similar scale for God's gender in rabbinic sources. The scholarship that focuses on rabbinic parables has by and large asserted God's exclusive maleness, not only in parables but across rabbinic sources.[6] To be certain, the overwhelming majority of rabbinic parables imagine God as male. This dominance of male God images, however, signals the very significance of the relatively few parables that dare to imagine, conflate, or even compare God with female figures. The novelty of these passages demands our attention. They invite us, as Psalm 45.11 did for Abraham in the parable above, to 'Hearken, O daughter, and see, and incline thine ear; forget also your own people, and your father's house'.

We do well to recall the parable about Israel as God's son and then female lover in the *Mekhilta* passage cited above. The end of that text reconfigured the Temple as the female lover's *mother's* house. The text thus gestures toward not only re-imagining God's Temple as the mother's house, where the female lover was conceived, but to imagine that God is also transformed into the mother of the House, and the one who conceives.

We also saw a parable above where Moses played God's wife, and mother of Israel. A 'proto'-parable reverses this dynamic as this text portrays Moses as God's husband:

'*This is the blessing, with which Moses the man of God blessed the people of Israel* (Deut 33.1) "Man of God" means husband of God.

Reish Lakish said, if it were not written it would be impossible to say: Just as a man decrees that his wife do something and she does it, so too, Moses decreed over God and God did it' (*Pesikta d'Rav Kahana Zot HaBrakhah* 1.13).

This text interprets Deuteronomy 33.1 quite literally. Man of God (*ish ha-elohim*) means Moses is God's husband. Moses plays the man, and thus God the wife/woman. Moses's maleness is constituted by virtue of his making a decree that his wife, God, must perform.

The final two parables I present offer relational matrices that are far less prevalent than king parables, and both are rooted in other domestic relationships than those of husband and wife. In both texts God is compared with or imagined as a female domestic worker. The first parable imagines God as a wet-nurse, who breast-feeds the infant Jacob.[7]

'R. Abbahu said, This is comparable to a son of kings who was sleeping in his cradle and there were flies settling on him. When his wet-nurse came, she bent over him and nursed him and the flies fled from him. So too, at first scripture states, *And behold, angels of God were ascending and descending on him [Jacob]* (Gen 28.12). When God revealed Godself to him, they fled from upon him' (*Genesis Rabbah* 69.3).

The second parable places the biblical figures of God, Jacob/Israel, and Moses in a complex web of family and domestic relationships. One of the more striking images the parable invokes is that of God as a female servant. The text interprets Exodus 3.11, 'And Moses said to God, Who am I [*anokhi*], that I should go to Pharaoh, and that I should bring the Israelites out of Egypt?'

'R. Joshua Ben Levi said: This is comparable to a king who married off his daughter and promised to give her a province and a female slave of high standing [*shifhah matrona*], but he gave her a female Cushite slave. His son-in-law said to him, "Didn't you promise to give to me a *shifhah matrona*?" So Moses said before the Holy Blessed One, "Master of the Universe, when Jacob went down to Egypt didn't you say to him, *I (anokhi) will go down with you into Egypt, and I [anokhi] will also bring you up again* (Gen 46.4). And now you say to me, '*So come, I will send you to Pharaoh*' (Ex 3.10). I am not the 'I' who said to him, 'I will also bring you up again'"' (*Exodus Rabbah* 3.4).

The parable in Exodus Rabbah 3.4 is the more complicated of the two, as the comparisons proliferate in a narrative space that presents gender as multiple and fluid rather than binary and rigid. Thus Jacob/Israel is the king's/God's daughter; she is married off by God, her father, who promises to give her a female slave as part of the marriage contract. Moses simultaneously plays the roles of husband of Israel, son-in-law of God, and female Cushite slave. Last but not least, God simultaneously embodies the roles of the king/father of Israel/father-in-law of Moses, and the female slave of higher standing. The shifting gendered roles throughout the parable reflect a complex, gendered narrative world that foregrounds gender fluidity and multiplicity over rigid, binary constructions of gender.

Taken together, the parables in this section have imagined God as a mother, a wife, a wet-nurse, and a female servant. They are indeed exceptional, far less prevalent than parables that portray God as king, father, or husband, but they nevertheless demonstrate that rabbinic parables disrupt a reading of God's gender as exclusively male. In parables, which are narratives saturated with theological import, part of what constitutes God is conceiving and breastfeeding Israel, protecting and delivering Israel, and serving Israel as a female servant. And, it is God as the female slave, moreover, who brings Israel out of Egyptian enslavement.

V Conclusion

Rabbinic parables have long been valued for their powerful, at times profound, theological insights. But their important contributions to deepening and refining our understanding of constructions of rabbinic gender have been far less common; those that do exist have framed parables as sites where binary gender is 'reversed', which still allows binary constructions of gender to define the terms within which rabbinic gender is set, and fixed. I have highlighted gender fluidity and multiplicity over and against the language of 'reversal' and its implicity binary framing in order to challenge the exclusive hold of binary gender in rabbinic parables specifically, and, given the prevalence of parables throughout rabbinic sources, rabbinic literature in general.

I have also highlighted connections between the performative nature of parables as stories and speech acts, and gender performativity. Performativity embeds and encodes within it the importance of 'doing', and I would add 'doings', 'undoings', and 're-doings'. If, as Jewish feminist theologian Rachel Adler so poignantly expressed, 'stories are the body of God',[8] rabbinic parables remind us that the bodies, and genders, of both God and Israel are as multiple and fluid as their theological import is enduring.

Notes

1. See David Stern, 'Imitatio Hominis: Anthropomorphism and the Character(s) of God in Rabbinic Literature', *Prooftexts*, 12.2 (1992), 151–174.
2. See Judith Butler, 'Performative Acts and Gender Consitution: An Essay in Phenomenology and Feminist Theory', *Theatre Journal*, 40.4 (1988); Judith Butler, *Gender Trouble: Feminism and the Subversion of Identity*, New York and London: Routledge, 1990.
3. Amy-Jill Levine, S*hort Stories by Jesus: The Enigmatic Parables of a Controversial Rabbi*, New York: HarperCollins Publishers, 2014, p. 4.
4. On the composition of collective Israel in the Hebrew Bible as referring to men specifically, not men and women, see Stuart MacWilliam, *Queer Theory and the Marriage Metaphor in the Hebrew Bible*, Sheffield: Equinox, 2011.
5. Phyllis Trible, 'Depatriarchalizing in Biblical Interpretation', *Journal of the American Academy of Religion* 41.1 (1973), 30–48.
6. Alan Appelbaum, *The Rabbis' King-parables: Midrash From the Third Century Roman Empire*. New Jersey: Gorgias Press, 2010, p. 175; Stern, 'Imitatio Hominis', pp. 163, 174.
7. See Numbers 11.12.
8. Rachel Adler, *Engendering Judaism: An Inclusive Theology and Ethics*, Boston: Beacon Press, 1998.

The Multiple Bodies of Jesus

CARMENMARGARITA SÁNCHEZ DE LÉON

Is the body of Jesus neutral, asexual? What sense can we make of a completely male Jesus? What impact does a Jesus with a closed-in maleness have on the lives of believing people, on the life of the Church or on theological thinking? Is it a he-body or she-bodies? If Jesus was totally human, perhaps we have good grounds for thinking that his incarnation is a becoming, never a finished process. In this becoming Jesus surprises us, distorts us, scandalises us.

I Introduction

Christianity was and is part of a civilising process that set out to tame whole populations. This taming process is a gag on the subversive and indecent content of the Gospels, to accentuate their patriarchal, colonial and excluding character. Jesus, as their central figure, has been stripped of much of his bodily integrity, his ambivalence, his development, to present us with a semi-god who calls us to sacrifice on behalf of the dominant powers. To act in conformity with the dominant powers is a 'decent life'.

As a consequence of the Spanish-American War of 1898, Puerto Rico, the Philippines, Guam and Cuba ceased to be subject to Spain and became territories under the control of the United States of North America. Puerto Rico was to remain permanently under North American administration. From the beginning of this invasion both the North American Protestant churches and the North American Catholic Church were part of this process of taming the Puerto Rican populations and imposing a firm Americanisation that from the perspective of the colonisers was the equivalent of the gospel itself.

Jesus' body as singular is a deformed body, designed to make us think that some of us have to adapt ourselves to this unique body, that our destiny is to live as objects of a patriarchal religion that not only censures the beauty of our bodily features but in addition makes us think that we do not deserve to live in dignity. This 'theological technology' results in the kidnapping of the indecent Jesus of the streets, the anti-system Jesus, and his turning into the lamb that was slain, the one whom especially the groups excluded by this patriarchal/colonial religion are supposed to imitate.[1]

II What is Christ's body like?

I think the picture is still there, just behind the main door of the church in Río Piedras, Puerto Rico, in the small lobby, an image of the face of Jesus Christ that has stayed in my mind to this day. A young man with light-coloured eyes, almost fair hair, slightly sunburnt. It was originally a charcoal sketch that the artist, Warner Sallman, turned into a painting. The Head of Christ or the Son of Man used to be in many Protestant homes and churches. For me it represents the limit of what the experience might mean: a white, North American man, sexless but sensual. Christ is located in terms of categories of power and privilege to which despicable bodies can have no access. Salvation is wrapped in categories and bodies that have to be stripped of their power before they can, in their nakedness, touch other bodies that have been oppressed and devalued.

The book *The Color of Christ: The Son of God and the Saga of Race in America* examines in depth the development of white subjectivities and the rise of the image of a white Jesus.[2] The image of the white Jesus was not present at every point of the history of the United States: this white Jesus was mocked by Mark Twain. Nonetheless, both at the height of slavery and at the rise of the United States as an imperial power, the image of the white Jesus emerges as the escort of white supremacy, male supremacy and imperial power. Thanks to the growing cinema industry, the United States succeeded in exporting this image of the white Jesus:

> As the United States rose to superpower status in the twentieth century, it also became the world's most active exporter of white Jesus imagery. Through film and art, American businessmen, moviemakers, and missionaries offered the world white Christ

figures to consume and worship.³

For feminist theologies and queer theologies, Christology is a problem. How can we be saved only by a male power? And from the perspective the theologies of the South we may add: how can we be saved not only by a man, but by a white one? Without losing sight of the fact that the biblical texts were written in fundamentally androcentric terms with a focus on the *kyrios*, the Lord, the theses of feminist theologies concentrate on finding elements that strip Jesus of absolute maleness. Part of this is recovering the concept of wisdom, the feminine spiritual force associated with Jesus, the prophet of Sophia. The other category that strips Jesus of hard maleness is his link with the community, which means non-hierarchical relationships and horizontal views. In this space – which Elisabeth Schüssler Fiorenza calls the *ekklesia* of women – we can abandon oppressive gender categories, even within the patriarchal system.

The model of an asexual Christ translates into path that insists on sacrifice as a fundamental virtue, a sacrifice strongly linked to the so-called 'pleasures of the flesh'. In our patriarchal societies this sacrifice is the toll the category women has to pay to be accepted. The web of hyperbole constructed around the lamb that was slain is labelled sacrificial religion by the Mexican theologian Carlos Mendoza-Álvarez. This sacrificial religion is imposed with great force on despised bodies, those that don't meet the standard, those that breach, contradict or distort the patriarchal capitalist system.

A couple of decades ago the Argentine theologian Marcella Althaus-Reid raised a warning flag about the danger of a theology done apart from bodies and sexualities. Because this theology will continue to reproduce the patriarchal model, she argued, we have to use new tools to look at our relationships and explore how, in future, we breathe divinity. Marcella identifies four criteria for 'reading' Christ:

1. Reading Christ in the scriptures cannot be an exemplary but a revelatory reading.
2. Reading Christ should not become a conclusive task.
3. Reading Christ needs to relate to Jesus' sexual practices. By that we understand Jesus' practices of solidarity with love and a praxis of social justice, outside a dualist mind/body separation.

4. Unless we can locate Jesus' passion in the real life of people we will not be able to understand the meaning of incarnation nor the subversion of bodies that resurrection implies.[4]

Marcella also invites us to read Christ with our imagination in those gaps in the text. Using these keys, we shall read and rethink Christology.

III Was he really a man?
Can we be really sure that Jesus was a man? Or did Jesus transition by changing himself? There are four moments in which we are told that Jesus changed his appearance: at his baptism (Lk 3.21-24), when he goes through a crowd without being recognised (Jn 8.56-59) and after the resurrection (Mk 16.1-12; Mt 28.16-17; Lk 24.13-43; Jn 20.11-18; Jn 21.1-14).

The dove, the divine Spirit, rests on Jesus and in this moment of being touched Jesus is transformed into the son of the dove. No-one seems to witness the moment, just the narrator. Jesus moves unnoticed through the people who came to John to be baptised, but not only is he one among many, but suddenly a dove moving through the people.

On Tabor three disciples are witnesses to the transformation of Jesus (Lk 9.28-36): he changes to an indescribable shape, he turns into another, perhaps light, perhaps air. The interesting thing is that this transfiguration is temporary, and so Jesus returns to his 'human' shape. The gospel of John describes the moment at which after a vigorous argument some people tried to stone Jesus. Jesus hides and it is as though he had turned into a different person; he moves through the people who had wanted to attack him and gets away without being recognised.

At various moments after Jesus' resurrection, he is not recognised by those with whom he had spent his time. Perhaps the most graphic account is the story of the disciples on the road to Emmaus: they spend considerable time with Jesus and don't recognise him until he breaks the bread. The gospels are an undefined genre that move from being accounts of the life of Jesus to reflections that try to explain a new faith conviction. Perhaps their richness lies in the fact that they are not attempts to catch the truth as a fixed object, but to communicate the message of Jesus and his ministry from different angles and so are flexible and contradictory.

Virginia Woolf's *Orlando* is a narrative presented as a fictional biography, though it contains verifiable information about Vita Sackville-

West. Vita, a conservative aristocratic writer, had been Woolf's lover. The plentiful contradictions in Sackville-West's life, the impossibility to find words to describe the experiences that crossed social barriers, gave Woolf enough material to imagine more than was sustainable. Orlando not only changed sex on various occasions, but this she/he would break the binaries because they could be 'read' as he/she/she/he in a continuing spiral. On the other hand, the spaces in the novel cannot be easily contained or limited, nor does the time seem to follow a linear logic. The breaches of oppressive, imposed social categories such as gender and sex, the logic of time and space, seem impossible to describe in words, and so imagination is required to be a text accompanying what we call truth.[5]

In a comparable way Jesus does not fit into the rigidity of fixed categories, but appears as a dove, light, woman, man, androgynous and sometimes contradicts himself, because he is annoyingly human.

IV I think Jesus is fat

The Gospels report that Jesus liked to eat and drink. He drank and ate especially with people who didn't have a good reputation. Our societies are in a complex struggle with food. On the one hand we are invited to enjoy food, but bodies are constantly measured to ensure that they maintain the right proportions. The pictures of Jesus I remember show a thinnish man, which doesn't match his enjoyment of spending time eating. Perhaps these pictures help to reinforce what the fat movement reminds us of: fat bodies are pathologised, presented as examples of being dirty and neglecting yourself, of what is incorrect and shouldn't be on show.

The Israeli comedian Yair Shlein reacted to doubts about the holocaust on the part of some Christians with a joke about Jesus, remarking that Jesus died at 40 because he was fat. I imagine the comedian knew the text of Mark's gospel in which Jesus says he was called a glutton. Shlein's joke didn't go down very well among the Christian community, but we don't know what caused most offence, the insinuation that Jesus didn't die on the cross or the reference to a shamefully fat body.

In 2011 in New York's Marlborough Gallery, the Colombian painter and sculptor Fernando Botero exhibited a collection of pictures entitled *Via Crucis*. The collection presents different scenes of the journey to the cross of a Jesus who is visibly fat. Although Botero has always worked with fat bodies, on the occasion of this exhibition he remarked that he was treating the subject with great respect and with no intention of satire. Why did he need to say this? Because the subject was Jesus or because Jesus was shown as fat? Erika Bülle-Hernández argues that:

> In this voracious struggle to obtain the ideal body without bothering about what it takes, society has created the need to present fat bodies as a spectacle and has played its part in discrimination against them. Bodies have in many cases decided to 'self-censure' what they do, and have given up completely their particular enjoyment and pleasures, destroying their freedom to have the body they want and turning some examples of people with fat bodies into an act of forced performativity, which, far from helping to give dignity and strength to this dissidence, puts the person's life at risk.[6]

The Filipino painter Emmanuel Garibay produced a series of paintings on the disciples on the road to Emmaus. They show Christ risen in the body of a slightly overweight voluptuous woman enjoying a table of good food and drink with her friends. We recognise her because she still has the marks of the nails on her hands. I think this female Christ is fat, but not in the pejorative sense that the system of body repression suggests to us. I think she's fat because she pulls me out of my balance, out of my comfort zone and leads me on to moving ground, to an area of uncertainty, and so Jesus becomes flesh in the fat, female, voluptuous and sensual Christ.

V The life of Brian

Over in the port of La Ceiba in Honduras lives Brian with his mummy. They say that this municipality in the Atlántico department was given this name because in these blessed lands there were many *ceiba* or kapok trees that kept the peace between heaven and earth. La Ceiba is one of the poorest regions in Honduras. The World Bank recognises that over 60 of Honduras' population live in poverty. UNICEF, the United Nations Children's Fund, notes that economic inequality in Honduras runs at one of the highest levels in the region, affecting especially children and women. In La Ceiba this inequality is even more acute, more graphic, more marked on the bodies exploited by an oppressive patriarchal capitalism. In this sense, poverty is porno-graphic and based on the low value the market gives to the despised bodies, which in one way or another are sold by capital.

One day Brian was playing in front of his house when a neighbour drove his car full-speed down the street. The car hit Brian. His desperate mother picked up his frail body and managed to find a taxi to take him to the hospital. Once they got there, the little Garífuna boy was taken and thrown on to a trolley like a piece of meat from the slaughter-house. The hospital staff told his mother that there was no point in treating him because Brian was going to die. She left the boy on the trolley for a short time while she went to beg the doctors to listen to her and admit the boy. When she came back she found the boy covered by a white sheet. Her screams of despair knew no bounds. At that moment a woman appeared from nowhere, took her hand and said: 'It's all right. Your son will live.' The mother says it was the voice of God. She regained her strength and bravely pleaded with the medical staff until her son was seen. Brian is alive, and for his mother it is proof that God is alive and hears, that God who was named ('the God who sees') by the slave woman Hagar (Gen 16.13).

Jesus is said to have been crucified on a tree trunk. The kapok trees of the Caribbean, whose branches spread wide, generally form a sort of cross, a cross like the letter T. These crosses are not symbols of death, but life, of the effort of the Maya and Garífuna communities to live to the full. Perhaps when Brian got back home, Jesus played the drum for the traditional *banguidi* or *punta* dance. This dance is kept for when an adult dies and goes over to their new life. Brian did not die, but came back to life, and possibly his mother danced the *punta*, swaying her hips in a seductive body prayer, thanking Jesus, who supported her with a woman's voice.[7]

VI There is a rumour...

During the time of the 'scorched earth' policy carried out for two decades by Guatemalan governments, the women of the Maya peoples were constantly victims of sexual assaults, enslavement and murder as part of an official policy of systematic genocide. The text *Tejidos que lleva el alma* bears witness to these horrendous actions against the Maya populations, but, even more importantly, bears witness to the resurrection of women dead while they lived.[8] For a long time the women who had suffered atrocities from the military kept silence, a silence rooted in shame at not having died. The silence was the grave in which they placed their bodies. But they were helped by other women to tell their stories in order to give a different meaning to the violence and emerge as resilient people. They succeeded in undoing the rumours with their accounts.

In a similar way, the synoptic gospels (Matthew, Mark and Luke) report that the first witnesses of the empty tomb were the women. In one of the accounts the women saw the empty tomb, but didn't say anything because they were afraid. Others talked about what had happened, but they were regarded as mad.

Tabitha, or Dorcas, was a woman of means, she made clothes for everyone, especially the widows. When Tabitha died, Peter came to Joppa and the widows met him in tears, and showed him the clothes Dorcas used to make for them.

The power of the three stories mentioned here lies in the community of women.

In Guatemala the women's support for each other was able to bring out from the murderous silence the women who had been victims of the army's barbarity, and although rumours started to go around that the 'living dead' had risen, many people would not believe it.

The widows Dorcas supported, in tears, showed Peter the clothes and he, impressed by the strength of the community, sends them all out of the room and prays. Tabitha comes back to life, raised, not by Peter's exclusivity, when he prays in private, but by the power of the women's lamentation, by the history told in the clothes that covered the widows' bodies.

Confronted by Jesus' empty tomb, some women were afraid, perhaps of what the authorities might do to them, but the silence did not last, just as it did not last in Guatemala, where, in an unprecedented move, with the support of other women, the victims went to court to give evidence of the murders and sexual violence, and were able to prove in court that the Rios Montt government had attempted genocide.

On that day Jesus began to rise in the thousands of disappeared because their histories were no longer a rumour but had become life.

VI By way of conclusion

Much has been done by the 'theological technologies' in an attempt to re-clothe Jesus and justify colonial or capitalist plans that oppress many people. Nonetheless Jesus allows himself to be stripped by she-bodies that bleed and menstruate, that dance and move their hips, fat, sensual bodies, she-bodies that rise again and again despite the deadly plans of the necro-powers.

Translated by Francis McDonagh

Notes

1. In the 1990s feminist theoreticians such as Teresa Lauretis adopted Michel Foucault's concept of biopower and created the concept of gender technology to explain how various cultural systems, universities, the cinema, literature, among others, nourish and support gender. I posit that theological activity has been and is part of this process of social construction. Theological technology derives from theological language, from the liturgy, pastoral ministry and biblical interpretation, and constructs a single way of living genders, sexuality and forms of bodiliness.
2. Edward J. Blum, *The Color of Christ: The Son of God and the Saga of Race in America*, Chapel Hill, NC, 2012.
3. Blum, *The Color of Christ*, p. 11.
4. Marcella Althaus-Reid, 'Mark', in Deryn Guest, Robert E. Goss, Mona West and Thomas Bohache (ed.), *The Queer Bible Commentary*, London, 2007, p. 516.
5. Sofía Falomir, 'El 'Orlando' de Woolf, y el método biográfico', *Acta Poética* 40.2 (2016), 53–73.
6. Erika Bülle Hernández, 'Cuerpos gordos: Empoderamiento a través de las prácticas performáticas', *Discurso Visual*, 42 (2018), 56–63.
7. https://www.youtube.com/watch?v=OmgPz6p0tNc.
8. Amandine Fulchirones (ed.), *Tejidos que lleva el alma*, Guatemala City, 2nd ed., 2011. The first edition is also available online: https://www.academia.edu/35293497/Tejidos_que_lleva_el_alma_Memoria_de_las_mujeres_mayas_sobrevivientes_de_violaci%C3%B3n_sexual_durante_el_conflicto_armado_Amandine_Fulchiron_coord._Angelica_Lopez_y_Olga_Alicia_Paz_F_and_G_Editores_Consorcio_Actoras_de_cambio_UNAMG_ECAP_Guatemala_2009

Ecclesiology: Becoming the Queer, Postcolonial, (Eco-)feminist Body of Christ in Asia

SHARON A. BONG

This paper offers an ecclesiological dimension to two forms of embodying a feminist-queer Christ in Asia: the Ecclesia of Women in Asia and the Free Community Church in Singapore that are intricately woven into the tapestry of Postcolonial, queer and (eco-)feminist theorizing and theologizing. The paper argues that to queer or make unfamiliar (theology, anthropology, Christology, ecclesiology, which are intertwined), necessarily restores and reconstitutes what had been lost, arguably perverted, but is now made tangible – an opening up and proliferation of possibilities of realizing a body of Christ who is redeemed by and for all in the here-and-now.

I Introduction

What does it mean to become church in Asia in the likeness of a queer Christ in the new millennium? On the one hand, the notion of queerness – that is suggestive of deviancy even perversion – seems alien to the commonly perceived conservatism of churches embedded in an Asian values system where Christianity comes largely as an effect of colonization (e.g. Spaniards in the Philippines, Portuguese in Malaysia, then Malaya, the Dutch in Indonesia, the British in India, and the French in China) and remains a minority faith (except in the Philippines and Timor-Leste). On the other hand, the notion of queerness – that is suggestive of disruption and multiplicity – resonates with the web of multi-cultural, multi-religious connections, ideological clashes and revolutions from below that characterize not only nationalist struggles in the past but also postcolonial endeavours of the present, e.g. political uprisings (e.g. Umbrella movement in Hong Kong), neo-liberalist market economies of Singapore and China amid the crippling poverty in South Asia (e.g. India, Bangladesh, Nepal), advocacy and outreach initiatives to mitigate the refugee crisis (e.g. Rohingyas in Myanmar), and gender-based violence faced by women and those with non-heteronormative genders and sexualities (e.g. death by stoning for those who commit adultery and gay sex in Brunei, the only Islamic State in Asia).

To queer, in essence (although there is no essential core to queerness), is to make strange (resist), to dismantle (deconstruct), and to reclaim (reconstruct). Within a Christian context, to queer the body of Christ, is to resist the overdetermined maleness of Christ; to deconstruct harmful dualisms that result from such androcentrism (e.g. male/female, mind/body, reason/emotion, white man/native other, heteronormative/non-heteronormative, Man/nature even human/non-human); and to reconstruct the human as made in the (queer) image of God – one that is *bodied* on mutuality, reciprocity and eroticism. This paper aims to offer an ecclesiological dimension to two forms of embodying a feminist-queer Christ in Asia, the Ecclesia of Women in Asia and the Free Community Church in Singapore, which are intricately woven into the tapestry of postcolonial, queer and (eco-)feminist theorizing and theologizing. The paper argues that to queer or make unfamiliar (e.g. theology, anthropology, Christology, ecclesiology, which are all intertwined), necessarily restores and reconstitutes what had been lost, arguably perverted, but is now made tangible – an opening up and proliferation of possibilities of realizing a body of Christ who is redeemed by and for all in the here-and-now.

II Beyond male/female

The liberating-salvific mission begins with the feminist project of dismantling the most fundamental dualism of all, that of male/female which is premised on the insistence of sexual difference as divinely-ordained hence natural law. As dualisms are hierarchically ordered (i.e. male as dominant and female as subjugated) and oppositionally related (i.e. female as non-male and by inference, inferiorized), the fixation of Christian thought and praxis on God the Father (theology) and the maleness of Christ (Christology), renders Man superior to Woman (anthropology).

The duality or polarity of ontological differences (i.e. equal but) and soteriological sameness (equality) between Man and Woman becomes the rock upon which the church is built. That human as created *imago dei* – albeit in the image of Father-God (rather than a genderless divine being) – compounds this duality and dualism. This in turn, renders gender complementarity of the sexes as a logical, expedient, natural order of creation; the Woman's *raison d'être* is as Man's complementary Other and helpmate. Man however, is not Woman's helpmate. Therein lies not only the non-reciprocal relations between the two but worse, a sexual hierarchy that logically, expediently and naturally becomes systematized as the structural sin of gender-based discrimination and violence against women in the home, in church, at the workplace, on the streets.

In this regard, the feminist hermeneutics of Elizabeth Schüssler Fiorenza is instructive in dismantling the dualism of male/female. Going back to the basics, through the example of the first century Christian communities, she revisits the pre-Pauline baptismal promise of Galatians 3.28 that is often touted (also by liberation, postcolonial and queer theologians) as biblical justification for the flattening of racial, class and sex differences: 'There is neither Jew nor Greek/ There is neither slave nor free/ There is no male and female'. Where Gnostics posit the ordinary figure of Man as androgynous, the apostle Paul insists on the '*symbolic* distinctions' (sexual difference) in place of 'functional distinctions' (gender roles). Schüssler Fiorenza, however, notes that in the last pair, unlike the other two (Jew/ Greek and free/slave), 'it does not speak of opposites but of man *and* woman'. With allusions to Genesis 1.27 where humanity is created in the image of God, 'qualified as "male and female"', she infers that the third pair 'does not assert that there are no longer men and women in Christ, but that patriarchal marriage – and sexual relationships between male and female – is no longer constitutive of the new community in Christ'. The 'egalitarian ethos of "oneness in Christ"' becomes the rock upon which the call to freedom (from biological determinism) and discipleship are extended to and taken up by women as women rather than 'becoming "male", "like man", and relinquishing her sexual powers of procreation'.[1] In calling into question the most fundamental of dualisms, male/female, she troubles two centuries of Church Fathers' perversion of egalitarian and inclusive sexual ethics that are already embedded in the heart (and loins) of Christianity.

Differences that matter – race, class, caste, sex – do not need to be erased or diminished in order to realize the mutuality rather than complementarity (which invariably marks the sexes differently and values man/woman disproportionately) that we are called to in the way we relate to each other. Schüssler Fiorenza, in borrowing from Jewish wisdom theology relevant to the early Christian communities, follows this relationality (rather than rationality) through in the radical vision and inclusive praxis of 'Sophia-God' and 'Jesus-Sophia' (wisdom) manifest in the discipleship of women as a 'discipleship of equals'.[2] Equality and inclusiveness become hallmarks of the first-century Jesus (messianic) movement of bountiful table-sharing with outcasts; the disinherited there-and-then, here-and-now. Prophet-like, she summons an *'ekklesia of women'* as a new model of becoming church: a '"new church" (as opposed to the 'patriarchal church') in solidarity with the oppressed and the "least" of this world', a religious-political gathering of women imbibed with the 'angry power' of Sophia-God who 'rejects the idolatrous worship of maleness' and 'internalization of the male as divine'. She counters predictable objections of 'reverse sexism' (as with 'reverse imperialism') by maintaining that 'mutuality with men' (as with mutuality with colonizers) can only be realized when the 'structural sin of sexism' (as with colonization) is brought down and the Church begins to heal from within when it has reconstructed itself.[3] This entails that the Church holds itself accountable, even repentant for the sins of its fathers, commits itself to revolutionary change in realizing the vision and mission of a 'discipleship of equals' (rather than the exclusivity of male clericalism) and stands in solidarity with (rather than persecution of) the 'least' among us.

In the light of this feminist, prophetic, and above all, Christian vision of becoming church not only in Asia but in the world, we are presented with a hollow version of this baptismal promise: the Study of the Diaconate of Women initiated by Pope Francis in 2016 that draws from the church's his-story of women deacons which rests on the affirmation of 'feminine genius' (itself premised on the principle of gender complementarity) first articulated by Pope John Paul II in his 'Letter to Women' in occasion of the 1995 Fourth UN World Conference on Women. These sit uneasily as half measures, a cop-out from the original intent, that all – (within the economy of) male and female – embody 'Sophia-God' and 'Jesus-Sophia' as members who profess the same faith. These stratagems are tantamount to relegating women to a messianic albeit sex-segregated table where the quality of the feast is perhaps second-rate (not unlike lower-grade food exports to developing countries) or where women and girls eat leftovers after the men and boys are done (an everyday reality of many women leading to their malnourishment). Son preference, which is so pervasive in the context of Asia (an ontological reality from womb to tomb, beginning with female infanticide), is mirrored in (rather than challenged by) the churches in Asia headed by an anthropomorphic male God that invests male privilege as a divinely-ordained birth right. A double perversion appears to be at work, depending on who is deciding this and for whom. The first is a purposeful and sustained deviation from the ethos of mutuality, equality and inclusiveness, and the second, a no less purposeful and sustained example of the 'structural sin' of ecclesiastical sexism.

At the heart of the exclusion of women from the priesthood or ecclesiastical leadership is a blindness that persists to exclude women on the basis of sex, as one who cannot embody (the maleness of) Christ because she lacks the male organ. Re-imagining the body of Christ beyond his whiteness – in effect, queering – is made familiar-but-not-quite through a de-colonizing lens by postcolonial theologians, as an Asian, flat-nosed Jesus with a third-eye. Re-imagining the body of Christ beyond his maleness – in effect, queering – is made familiar-but-not-quite through a transgressive lens by feminist-queer theologians, as *Christa*, the female Christ, 'who undresses the masculinity of God', Christ 'as a poor prostitute' who is triply oppressed by virtue of her race, class and sex,[5] Christ as 'mother, woman and shaman', whose life-giving blood is that of Christ brutalized at the Cross, in the name of God the Father, and for the sake of humankind.[6] In unmasking the imperialism of a life-taking theology that reduces female bodies and bodily experiences as less worthy or more defiled, an 'incarnational body theology' that begins with the concrete, messy realities of surviving or aspiring to live abundantly, that seeks to 'reflect on (all) body experiences as revelatory of God'[7] is more faithful to the baptismal promise long withheld from half the human race, and others. Pregnant bodies (which includes women and now, female-to-male transgender persons who delay their transitioning)[8] in all their potentiality for reproductive fecundity maybe a repugnant figure at the altar to some but are surely the full (in more senses than one) embodiment of Christ as co-equal creators and paradigmatic embodiment of Sophia-God.

'In memory of her' represents not only biblical women who led the way (for those who intentionally lost the way for others), wo/men whose bodies suffer, resist and heal, but also the 'least' among us and all who take on the 'angry power' of Sophia-God to engender a heaven on earth for all, founded on a relationality that is socially just and lovingly inclusive. In memory of her, the Ecclesia of Women in Asia (EWA), a gathering of Catholic-feminist women theologians, sought to break the silence of (religious and lay) theologians from the womb of Asia whose voices were not hitherto heard. EWA 'expresses the desire of women to enter the mainstream Church as fully responsible ecclesial participants and partners in the life of the Church. EWA seeks to bring to consciousness that women are Church and always have been Church'.[9] In memory of her, gathering the voices of the silenced who have been violated by clergy and the complicity of popes, archbishops and bishops – as abuses of the excesses of male privilege – is to stand in solidarity with survivors of gender-based violence and to speak out against those who continue to wound because they can.[10]

III Beyond heteronormative/non-heteronormative

The liberating-salvific mission continues with the queer project of dismantling the corollary dualism to male/female which is heteronormative/non-heteronormative, premised on the insistence of heterosexuality as divinely-ordained hence natural law. As dualisms are hierarchically ordered (i.e. heterosexuality as normal and non-heterosexuality as abnormal) and oppositionally related (i.e. non-heteronormativity as deviating from the norm of heterosexuality and consequently, marginalized, pathologised, even demonized), the fixation of Christian thought and praxis on the rightness of heterosexuality renders heterosexuals morally superior to non-heteronormative persons, e.g. gay or lesbian-identifying persons, bisexuals, transgender or intersex persons and those who are queer (e.g. asexual, pansexual, gender fluid) or questioning (LGBTIQ+). The ontological differences are fixed (flawed non-heteronormative persons are not quite created in the perfection of a presumed heterosexualized image of God). And soteriological sameness (equality) may be achieved through celibacy, i.e. not acting on one's sexual desires (where loving the sinner but not the sin, is as good as it gets in terms of pastoral care of LGBTIQ+ persons in mainstream churches). This becomes the rock upon which traditional family values and the Church's sexual ethics are built. That 'Church Fathers took the lived reality of [...] [the] enfleshed first-century rabbi [...] [and turned it into] the virginal and celibate Son of God'[11] compounds the metaphysical mind/body split (aligned with the male/female dualism or binary). This leads to body dysmorphic disorders (a dis-embodying) within the divine/human body, often resulting in shame, guilt and pain among LGBTIQ+ persons.

The Church's body theology that naturalizes gender binaries and heteronormativity leads to Church-sponsored sex-negative and harmful messages and practices. Examples include conversion therapies for LGBTIQ+ persons (to cast out the demon of homosexuality), Abstinence-only-until-marriage sexuality education programmes, withdrawal of state funds for Abstinence+ programmes or comprehensive sexuality education that offer sex-positive messages which include bodily integrity, safer sex practices, knowledge of contraceptives to facilitate informed decisions about one's sexual reproductive health and rights. Gender-based violence directed at LGBTIQ+ persons, e.g. hate crimes fuelled by homophobia and transphobia (fear and hatred of gay-identifying and transgender persons), corrective rape, often at the behest of parents of LGBTIQ+ persons, go uncorrected. All bodies and sexualities are policed to ensure conformity to discursive practices (which is the general aim of the Church's body theology) that affirm what Judith Butler calls the 'heterosexual matrix'[12] – the neat alignment of one's sex/gender/desire (e.g. if one is born male, one ought to be gendered masculine and desire the opposite sex). This is the one natural rule that all should obey – happy are those who fit in and woe to those who do not! Bodies and sexualities, especially of LGBTIQ+ persons that cannot be straight-jacketed or resist being heterosexualized, find expression instead through 'gender performativity' – reflected in the lived realities of myriad combinations of sexual orientation, gender identity and expression, and sexual characteristic (SOGIESC). That *gender* is not a noun [...] gender is always doing' makes visible the inexhaustible gender work involved in constructing these categories as fixed and stable.[13] In effect, this means that one is not born but becomes heterosexual – dismantling gender binaries de-naturalizes the (un)learning and (un)doing of SOGIESC for all.

How does the body of Christ fit into such transgressive modes? How are the bodily experiences of LGBTIQ+ persons revelatory of God's splendour and grace? Welcoming LGBTIQ+ persons to the bountiful messianic table – as a moral and political imperative – entails challenging the Church's heterosexism, i.e. systemic and systematic discrimination, even demonization of LGBTIQ+ persons. It also involves re-imagining the body of Christ beyond 'his' presumed heterosexuality, virginity and celibacy – in effect, queering – which paradoxically renders Christ quite familiar to LGBTIQ+ persons albeit a stranger to others. In a queer body of Christ, LGBTIQ+ persons see the messy materiality of their body realities (blood, sweat, tears, semen and vaginal discharges) reflected and see that it is good – the profane becomes sacred. According to James B. Nelson, although Christianity confines 'the divine reincarnation exclusively to Jesus' (thus giving rise to 'Christian triumphalism', i.e. only those who believe and fit in, will be saved), 'Christians can see other incarnations: the *christic* reality expressed in other human beings in their God-bearing relatedness'. He adds that, 'the marvellous paradox is that Jesus empties himself of claims to be the exclusive embodiment of God, and in that self-emptying opens the continuing possibility for all other persons'.[14] The '*christic* reality' of suffering, resistance and healing experienced by LGBTIQ+ persons extends the redemptive grace poured out through Christ's *kenosis* (self-emptying), life-giving love for all, and above all, the 'least' among us. In this way, Christ was always already queered – the sacred becomes profane.

Queer theologies and Christology in this regard push the porous boundaries between divine/human and sacred/profane to indecent limits. Queer theologians offer counter-narratives that seek to redeem, paradoxically by subverting the body of Christ for all. They do so firstly by proliferating the '*christic* reality' expressed in LGBTIQ+ persons 'in their God-bearing relatedness' and secondly, as feminist theologians have done, by reclaiming the power of the erotic. Marcella Althaus-Reid travels down the 'path of obscenity, as a methodology, to find more radical per/versions of Christ' – material and multiple meanings beyond the corset and closet of a 'Monotonous Mono/Christ' (heterosexualized, virginal, celibate) to a 'Bi/Christ' that reflects the sense of how LGBTIQ+ persons are bodied – how they look, how they smell, how they touch and feel.[15] 'Take back Jesus', Kittridge Cherry advocates, for '[n]obody owns the copyright on Christ', as she traces queer Christian art complete with leatherdykes engaged in BDSM practices (bondage/discipline, dominance/submission, sadism/masochism).[16]

The fear and hatred of women and the feminine are profoundly related to a fear of the erotic or erotophobia that remains a colonizing weapon used to oppress by repressing (i.e. marking as different and valuing as inferior) the feminized other, e.g. women, emotion, the body, indigenous peoples and the earth, as articulated by queer eco-feminists.[17] As such, dismantling the intersecting dualisms of male/female, mind/body, reason/emotion, white man/native other, heteronormative/non-heteronormative, Man/nature even human/non-human, entails, among other subversive tools, reclaiming the redemptive power of the erotic. Althaus-Reid laments the legacy of systematic theologians who have constructed a 'de-eroticised' and 'lustless messiah', sanitized through the filtering process (dualism) of embodying either agapian or erotic love.[18] For Carter Heyward, '[o]ur power is erotic because it is about embodying relational connections'. The profundity of this relational movement powered by the erotic is embodied not only in 'erotically empowered/empowering women' but also in Christa, who 'moves among us in our right relatedness […] the power by which we know ourselves to be a commonpeople'.[19]

The erotic power of relationality, present among the 'commonpeople'-'discipleship of equals' celebrates a shared sexual ethics of mutuality, equality and inclusiveness. At the heart of this troubling, playful erotic power is the loving call to extend hospitality to the stranger within and among us for in these bodies, Christ resides. The call is taken up by the Free Community Church (FCC) in Singapore which is an LGBTIQ+-friendly sacred and safe space for all, as it 'affirms that all individuals, including lesbian, gay, bisexual and transgender persons, are individuals of sacred worth created in God's image'. The FCC also 'affirms that same-sex and transgender relationships, when lived out in accord with the love commandments of Jesus, are consistent with Christian faith and teachings […] [and] find discrimination based on negative judgment of others, fear of difference, and homophobia inconsistent with Christian teachings'. The *imago dei* through the body of Christ is thus redeemed for and by all who thirst, are hungry and seek shelter in the bosom and loins of Christ-Sophia-God.

IV Conclusion

The body of Christ is queer in transgressing not only axes of differentiations such as gender, sexuality, class but also life/death. Doing church involves the realization that the liberating-salvific mission continues with the queer project of dismantling the dualisms of male/female: the Ecclesia of Women in Asia that is premised on a "discipleship of equals". The queer project, indeed praxis, also calls to question the dualism of heteronormative/non-heteronormative: the Free Community Church. Doing church in these ways embodies a feminist-queer Christ that dwells in Asia that in challenging the structural and systemic sins of sexism and homophobia is not only restorative but also transformative in realizing a body of Christ who is redeemed by and for all in the here-and-now.

Notes

1. Elisabeth Schüssler Fiorenza, *In Memory of Her: A Feminist Theological Reconstruction of Christian Origins*, New York: Crossroad, 1983, pp. 204, 211, 218.
2. Schüssler Fiorenza, *In Memory of Her*, pp. 132, 135.
3. Schüssler Fiorenza, *In Memory of Her*, pp. 344, 346–347.
4. Choan-Seng Song, *Third-Eye Theology: Theology in Formation in Asian Settings*, Guildford and London: Lutterworth Press, 1980.
5. Marcella Althaus-Reid, *Indecent Theology: Theological Perversions in Sex, Gender and Politics*, London and New York: Routledge, 2000, pp. 111, 122.
6. Chung Hyun Kyung, *Struggle to Be the Sun Again: Introducing Asian Women's Theology*, Maryknoll: Orbis Books, 1990, pp. 64–69.
7. James B. Nelson, *Body Theology*, Louisville, Kentucky: Westminister/John Knox Press, 1992, p. 51.
8. Henry Bodkin, 'Sex-Change Men "Will Soon Be Able to Have Babies"', *The Telegraph*, 4 November 2017, at: https://www.telegraph.co.uk/news/2017/11/04/babies-born-transgender-mothers-could-happen-tomorrow-fertility/.
9. See the homepage of EWA at: https://ecclesiaofwomen.com.
10. Carol Glatz, 'Survivors Speak: What Vatican Summit Must Do to Stop Abuse', *Catholic Philly*, 20 February 2019, at http://catholicphilly.com/2019/02/news/world-news/survivors-speak-what-vatican-summit-must-do-to-stop-abuse/.
11. Lisa Isherwood, 'Sexuality and the "Person" of Christ', in Lisa Isherwood and D. von der Horst (eds.), *Contemporary Theological Approaches to Sexuality*, London and New York: Routledge, 2018, p. 277.
12. Judith Butler, *Gender Trouble: Feminism and the Subversion of Identity*, New York and London: Routledge, 1990, p. 280.
13. Butler, *Gender Trouble*, p. 285.
14. Nelson, *Body Theology*, pp. 51–52.
15. Althaus-Reid, *Indecent Theology*, pp. 112, 118.
16. Kittredge Cherry, 'Take Back Jesus: The Queer Christ Arises for the Good of All',

Tikkun, 23.2 (2008), 48–50.
17. Greta Gaard, 'Toward a Queer Ecofeminism', *Hypatia*, 12.1 (1997), p. 132. doi: 10.2979/HYP.1997.12.1.114
18. Althaus-Reid, *Indecent Theology*, p. 120.
19. Carter Heyward, *Touching Our Strength: The Erotic as Power and the Love of God*, New York: HarperCollins Publishers, 1989, pp. 20, 115–116.
20. See the homepage of FCC at: https://www.freecomchurch.org

'Can Anything Good Come from Nazareth? Come and see!' An Invitation to Dialogue Between Queer Theories and African Theologies

NONTANDO HADEBE

Emerging queer theologies in Africa have to contend with the question of how various identities (African, Christian, queer etc.) can be brought together. Hence this article draws on the conversation between Philip and Nathaniel (Jn 1.45–46) where prejudice ('Can anything good come from Nazareth?') is met with an invitation ('Come and see'), culminating in a transformative encounter with Jesus. This invitation will be proposed as a framework for a dialogue between queer theories and African theologies.

I Introduction

'Like coal miners used caged canary birds, whose death was a warning sign of toxic gases in the mine tunnels, homosexual women and men, and transgender and intersex people in southern Africa are at the coalface of the multiple dangers in many of our societies today. How our societies treat lesbian, gay, bisexual, transgender and intersex (LGBTI) people is symptomatic of the dangers facing all people who are excluded in some way or another in our societies, by those who have a grip on social, economic, and political power.'[1]

The above quotation makes responsible those with a 'grip on social, economic and political power' for the 'multiple dangers' faced by LGBTI persons and other marginalized groups. These violations are essentially 'identity wars' because the only criterion for being subjected to multiple violations is one's belonging to a particular group. African theologians, too, are no strangers to 'identity wars' because one of the first challenges to which they had to respond was whether African identity was consistent with being Christian; in other words, could one be 'African' and 'Christian'? LGBTI persons face the same question of whether they can remain true to their sexual identity and still be Christian and African. Is it possible to claim a triple identity as queer, Christian and African? Homophobic positions will argue that it is impossible to possess this triple identity, and hence as mentioned in the quotation, queer persons face multiple forms of violence. However, as the quotation also notes, these violations are not exclusively faced by queer persons but also by other marginalized groups. By implication, responding to queer experiences translates into addressing the fundamental causes underlying identity-based conflicts that are destroying many parts of Africa and are also creating fragmentation in the Church. Queer theory's critique of structures and practices of exclusion provides an important resource for a dialogue between queer theory and African theologies that aims at social transformation and liberation of sexual *and* other minorities.

Queer theory disrupts and problematizes fixed essentialist identities such as homosexuality, heterosexual, ethnicity, and proposes fluid and diverse identities. Yet, there may be scepticism on whether there is merit in engaging with queer theory. Hence my appropriation of the dialogue between Philip and Nathaniel which starts with resistance ('Can anything good come from Nazareth?') and continues with an invitation ('Come and see'), culminating in a transformative encounter with Jesus (Jn 1.47–56). My proposal for a dialogue between queer theory and African theology draws on the four characteristics of queer theory outlined by Patrick S. Cheng.[2] But before discussing queer theory in dialogue with African theologies, I will briefly offer some context on the status of queer persons in some parts of Africa.

II Context: The status of queer persons in some parts of Africa
Decolonial theorists argue that identities in former colonies cannot be

understood apart from the colonial legacies that legitimized and sustained inequality. Ramón Grosfoguel[3] describes the colonial 'power matrix' as consisting of fifteen global hierarchies that privilege some groups at the expense of others, for example 'a sexual hierarchy that privileges heterosexuals over homosexuals and lesbians'; 'a global racial/ethnic hierarchy that privileges European people over non-European people'; and 'a spiritual hierarchy that privileges Christians over non-Christian/non-Western spiritualities institutionalized in the globalization of the Christian (Catholic and later, Protestant) church.'[4] Colonial law criminalized homosexual acts and was supported by Christian beliefs. In Catholicism, for example, we find both the affirmation of the dignity of LGBTIQ persons as created in the image of God[5] and the strong condemnation of homosexual acts as 'intrinsically disordered.'[6] Similarly, popular discourses by politicians claim that homosexuality is 'un-African and an import from the Western countries'.[7] These colonial, legal and religious legacies have contributed to homophobia in many parts of Africa, resulting in a situation where LGBTI persons experience multiple forms of violence in public and private spaces:

> 'The last decade has seen an unprecedented rise in the levels of discrimination and violence directed towards lesbian, gay, bisexual, transgender and intersex (LGBTI) people in sub-Saharan Africa. LGBTI people have faced harassment, persecution, and vilification. They have been subject to: forcible eviction from their homes because of who they are; being kicked out of churches and schools; laws that have been introduced to introduce or increase sanctions for consensual same-sex sexual activity; arbitrary arrest by police; imprisonment for actual or suspected consensual same-sex conduct (or for their identities); torture and other ill treatment whilst in detention; judicially-ordered forced anal examinations; murder; rape; beatings; stabbings; being branded paedophiles; accused of "recruiting" children into homosexuality; accused of sorcery; disowned by their own families; public denigration by politicians and political parties; and blame by religious leaders for societies' economic and social ills. This is not an exhaustive list.'[8]

These acts of terror and brutality against queer persons are an indictment of the societies in which they take place as well as the religions that are part of these societies. As mentioned in the introduction, other forms of identity-based discrimination and resulting violent conflicts have destroyed many lives through genocides, xenophobia, inter-religious wars, and political violence based in ethnicities. In these contexts of identity-based violence, can queer theory's critique of identity categories provide an alternative framework for constructing identities and peaceful and just societies?

III Four Characteristics of Queer Theory

In his review of the contribution of queer theory to theology, Patrick Cheng offers a summary of four main characteristics of queer theories, namely identity without essence; transgression; resistance to binaries; and social construction. I will briefly present these before discussing their contributions to the dialogue between queer theory and African theologies.

a) Identity without essence

Queer theory criticizes 'stable identity markers' and their claims to 'naturalness.' It resists the essentialism that characterizes fixed identities of sexuality, race or gender and the forms of oppression based on these categories. Queer theory is a way of thinking whose critique of identity categories is not confined to gender and sexual identities but also includes categories that create difference, such as race, class and ethnicities.[9] It examines the underlying power structures that construct difference as inequality which, as noted in the previous section, is implicated in human rights violations not only of LGBTI person but of all marginalized groups.

b) Transgression

Transgression in the context of queer theories refers to the commitment to challenge 'the normal, the legitimate and dominant'.[10] Therefore 'to queer' as a verb refers to actions that 'subvert, deconstruct and challenge' the status quo rather than reaffirm any position. For oppressed groups, the 'normal and legitimate' are constructions that are used by those in power to legitimize and sustain inequality. Thus queer theory is in synch with liberation movements that start with the concrete, lived experiences of injustice of oppressed groups as the framework that empowers them to rename, resist and oppose the oppressive social systems legitimized by the powerful.

c) Resistance to binaries

Queer theories destabilize and resist binaries, for example the gender binary that divides humanity in female and male, that are absolutized, essentialized and homogenized without the recognition of diversity among individuals or the existence of groups that do not identify exclusively with either sex, such as gender-fluid or intersex persons. Binaries are the source of inequality when one part is valued higher than the other and are thus at the base of power structures. This is true also for other binary ways of categorization including race (white and black), ability (disabled and able-bodied), ethnicity (African and non-African) and human and rest of creation.[11]

d) Social construction

The theory of social construction is central to queer theory and its liberative emphasis because it demystifies the assumption that identities are 'natural' and points to human agency working together with other social and historical forces in the construction and development of identities over time and in different contexts. Because socially constructed, identity-based oppressive can be deconstructed, resisted and reconstructed.

Homophobia is a barrier to dialogue with queer theories; therefore a model of invitation as a response to resistance will be discussed next.[12]

IV Invitation in Response to Resistance

As noted earlier, the dialogue between Philip and Nathaniel that is characterized by resistance and invitation is proposed as the starting point for the dialogue between queer theories and theologies in Africa. This, however, does not imply that African theologians are not already critically engaging with homophobia, but rather that there is not much dialogue with western queer theories so far. I will use the text from the Gospel of John as a narrative that becomes a metaphor for dialogue, and therefore will not develop an exegetical analysis of the text.

Let me quote from John 1.43–50:

'The next day Jesus decided to go to Galilee. He found Philip and said to him, "Follow me." Now Philip was from Bethsaida, the city of Andrew and Peter. Philip found Nathaniel and said to him, "We have found him about whom Moses in the law and also the prophets wrote, Jesus son of Joseph from Nazareth." Nathaniel said to him, *"Can anything good come out of Nazareth?" Philip said to him, "Come and see."* When Jesus saw Nathaniel coming toward him, he said of him, "Here is truly an Israelite in whom there is no deceit!" Nathaniel asked him, "Where did you get to know me?" Jesus answered, *"I saw you* under the fig tree before Philip called you." Nathaniel replied, "Rabbi, you are the Son of God! You are the King of Israel!" Jesus answered, "Do you believe because I told you that I saw you under the fig tree? *You will see greater things than these.*"' [my emphasis]

Three aspects of the narrative will be discussed: the naming of the characters' cities of origin as a source of prejudice; resistance and invitation; and the encounter with Jesus. First, it is interesting to note that the city of Bethsaida is associated with Philip, Andrew and Peter, which seems to indicate a positive quality of the city and its inhabitants. Jesus is identified through Nazareth, the city where he was raised. These identity markers attribute status to particular locations, and in this case Nazareth and everybody from there are portrayed negatively as 'lacking any good,' a sign of the marginalization of Nazareth. Second, Nathaniel's instinctive response to Phillip's description of Jesus as the Messiah from Nazareth reflects the prevailing social prejudice associated with the city and its inhabitants. Philip does not argue but invites Nathaniel to come and witness someone from Nazareth who does not fit the stereotype. Surprisingly Nathaniel offers no resistance and accompanies Philip to meet Jesus, an encounter that disrupts everything that he believed about people from Nazareth. Third, in his response to Nathaniel, Jesus does not refer to any identity markers or prejudice but instead addresses him as an individual focusing on his character ('in whom there is no deceit') and specific action ('sitting under a fig tree'). During their conversation free from prejudice and stereotypes, Nathaniel encounters Jesus in his true identity as the 'Son of God.' Their recognition of each other's true identities brings about a new reality that transcends their identities contained in Jesus' promise that Nathaniel will see 'greater things than these.' This narrative includes strands of queer theory, such as the breaking down of fixed identities (Nazareth versus Bethsaida), transcending and transgressing binaries (Jesus's non-discriminatory conversation with Nathaniel) and the move beyond identities toward the transformation of society, reflected in Jesus' mission throughout the gospels and summarized in Luke 4.17-19. Hence this narrative offers a framework for dialogue between queer theories and African theologies.

V 'Come and See': African Theologies and Queer Theories

As mentioned above, African theologies emerged from the resistance to the identity crisis of being both African and Christian. The dominant colonial narrative emphasized 'the notion that non-Europeans differ utterly and essentially from Europeans was a cornerstone of colonialist thought'.[13] Many missionaries shared these colonial beliefs and it was this 'ideological identification of the missionary enterprise with the colonial regimes that generated a crisis of identity amongst the African converts'.[14] Further, some missionaries denigrated African cultures which made it 'inconceivable to them that there could be anything positive in these cultures through which the gospel message might be conveyed'.[15] Similarly, apartheid in South Africa used the Bible to legitimize racism.

In the dialogue that I initiate here as a response to the experience of the rejection of queer persons, I will draw on the characteristics of queer theories described by Cheng that are also reflected in the narrative from the gospel of John to show how these can help to provide a theological response to identity-based conflict, violence and discrimination that continue to plague many parts of Africa. Identity categories also plays a role in the Catholic Church as criteria for inclusion and exclusion. For example, marital status, sexual identity and denomination are markers used to exclude persons from communion (divorced and remarried persons, non-Catholics) or ordination (women, married men, queer persons).

In order to begin this dialogue, I will discuss two points central to queer theory, namely the transgression of binaries and fixed identities, and the transcendence of identities as acts of social justice.

First, queer theory disruption and transgression of binaries that perpetuate fixed identities by creating fluid and diverse identities is an act of social justice because differences among groups are often used by those in power to justify discrimination and exclusion resulting violence and conflicts. For example, ethnic conflicts are sustained by fixed identities that enable group members to identify those within and outside their group. It is not uncommon in daily interactions for people to refer to persons exclusively in terms of their ethnicity. For example, many people think, 'he or she is (name of ethnic group) and that is why they behave in a particular way or possess a particular characteristic'. This identity is perceived to be constant and present in all members of the group. The genocide in Rwanda is a tragic example of the destructive power of fixed identities. In the narrative from John, Nathaniel's initial resistance to Jesus was based on such collective identities associated with geographical location. Hence, the call of queer theory for fluid, non-binary and diverse identities has the potential to break down the walls that divide groups and confine individuals to a particular collective identity. Fluid identities allow for diversity that liberates group members and hopefully generate acceptance of diversity in all groups. As seen in the conversation between Jesus and Nathaniel, the dissolution of rigid identities can result in encounters free of prejudice and stereotype, where authentic individual identities emerge. Similarly, the disruption of rigid binary identity categories in the Catholic Church could lead to an inclusive community from which nobody is excluded on the basic of their identity. The shift from fixed binary identities to fluid diverse identities will require theological anthropologies that foster just relationships and practices. Trinitarian theology provides an important resource because within the Trinity of Father, Son and Holy Spirit we find difference, equality, relationship and oneness. Leonard Boff describes a trinitarian anthropology as follows,

> 'In the Trinity there is no domination by one side, but convergence of the Three in mutual acceptance and giving. They are different but none is greater or lesser, before or after. Therefore a society that takes its inspiration from Trinitarian communion cannot tolerate class differences, dominations based on power (economic, sexual or ideological) that subjects those who are different to those who exercise that power and marginalizes the former from the latter.'[16]

Another resource is the African concept of personhood as relational and communal. For example, in my language, *Ndebele*, we say *umuntu ngumuntu ngabantu* (a persons is a person because or through others). Elias Bogmba describes *ubuntu* as 'humaneness': 'central to the concept is the idea that relations and transactions that take place among people should be undertaken humanely, in the light of values people share in a given community'.[17]

The second aspects proceeds from the first, and asks whether we need identity categories at all given that they have been the source of conflict, discrimination and injustice? Queer theory is justifiably wary that newly established fluid identities could with time become fixed and reproduce similar prejudices and conflicts. Hence the need for a flow of identities that are constantly critiqued, evolving and resisting fixations. An example of this is a comparison of pre-independence and post-independence experiences of identity in colonized Africa. During the struggle against colonialism there was one singular shared identity of being an 'African' or a national of one's country. After independence, this fixed identity was challenged by those who felt excluded, such as minority ethnic groups, women, persons with disabilities and queer persons. These groups developed a collective identity in order to fight a common cause but with time, the differences within these groups disrupted their identity, and the process of continues. This process of disruption is an issue of justice because it seems that as soon as identities are fixed there is exclusion of other groups followed by injustice and conflict. Queer theory's insistence that the way to justice is the constant disruption of identity categories is supported from a practical perspective by such struggles for liberation. Therefore queer theory is a quest for social justice which, when integrated with theology, produces liberation theologies that promote justice in church and society.

VI Conclusion

Queer theory disrupts, transgresses and transcends identities as an act of social justice. The narrative in John shows us a conversation that confronts and disrupts prejudice in an encounter that reveals the personhood of Jesus and Nathaniel outside of group identities. This transcendence of identities promises to be the gateway for a vision of social justice reflected in the words and deeds of Jesus. Inspired by this conversation, my proposal for a dialogue that draws on the insights of queer theory, integrating trinitarian theological anthropology and African traditions of personhood, offers alternative resources for addressing identity-based conflicts and violations of human rights currently taking place in many parts of Africa, as well as practices of exclusion and inclusion in the Catholic Church. The contributions of queer theory are critical for both church and society not only in Africa but in the world.

Nontando Hadebe

Notes

1. Mark Gevisser, *Canaries in the Coal Mines: An analysis of Activism of Spaces for LGBTI Activism in Southern Africa*, Johannesburg: Other Foundation, 2016, p. 3, at http://theotherfoundation.org/canaries-in-the-coal-mines/.
2. Patrick S. Cheng. 'Contributions from Queer Theory', in Adrian Thatcher (ed.), Oxford *Handbook of Theology, Sexuality and Gender*, Oxford: Oxford University, 2015, pp. 154–169.
3. Ramón Grosfoguel, 'Decolonizing Post-Colonial Studies and Paradigms of Political-Economy: Transmodernity, Decolonial Thinking, and Global Coloniality', *Transmodernity: Journal of Peripheral Cultural Production of the Luso-Hispanic World*, 1.1, at https://escholarship.org/uc/item/21k6t3fq.
4. Grosfoguel, 'Decolonizing Post-Colonial Studies'.
5. Pope Francis, *Joy of Love*, at https://w2.vatican.va/content/dam/francesco/pdf/apost_exhortations/documents/papa-francesco_esortazione-ap_20160319_amoris-laetitia_en.pdf.
6. *Catechism of the Catholic Church*, no. 2357, at http://www.vatican.va/archive/ENG0015/_INDEX.HTM.
7. Gevisser, Canaries in the Coal Mines.
8. Amnesty International, 'Speaking Out: Advocacy Experiences and Tools of LGBTI Activists in Sub-Saharan Africa', 2014, at ttps://www.amnesty.org/en/documents/afr01/001/2014/en/.
9. Cheng, 'Contributions from Queer Theory', p. 156.
10. Cheng, 'Contributions from Queer Theory', p. 156.
11. Cheng, 'Contributions from Queer Theory', p. 157.
12. Cheng, 'Contributions from Queer Theory', p. 156.
13. Jürgen Osterhammel, *Colonialism: A Theoretical Overview*. Translated from German by Shelley L. Frisch, Princeton: Markus Wiener Publishers, 1997, p. 107.
14. Jesse N.K. Mugambi, *Christianity and African Culture*, Nairobi: Acton Publishers, 2002, p. 2.
15. Diane Stinton. 'Africa, East and West,' in John Parratt, *Introduction to Third World Theologies*, Cambridge: Cambridge University Press, 2004, pp. 105–136.
16. Leornado Boff, *Trinity and Society*. Translated from Portuguese by Paul Burns, Oregon: Wipf and Stock, 1988, p. 151.
17. Elias K. Bogma, 'Reflections on Thabo Mbeki's African Renaissance', *Journal of Southern African Studies*, 30.2 (2004), 298.

Love in the Last Days: The Eschatological Marking of Bodies Resembling an Infinitely Queer Desire

ÁNGEL F. MÉNDEZ-MONTOYA

The complexities of the meaning of 'queering' as a body that is inclusive, dynamic and eschatological (in constant development) spark some theological reflections mentioned here briefly and rather piecemeal.

I Undoing dominant violent body semiotics

Before gaining currency in the academic world, *queer* theory came in off the streets, surrounded by a sea of sexually and gender diverse bodies shouting as one: 'We're here and we're queer. Get used to it!' Bodies of lesbians, gays, bisexuals, transvestites, transsexuals, transgender and intergender people (LGBTTTI), marching in the streets to resist the constant use of a humiliating and dehumanising label that led to socio-political and religious practices that stripped human rights and human dignity from this *queer* body that 'now' raised its voice to announce that it was 'here'.[1] In this article 'queer', like the Spanish coinage *cuir*, also designates subordinate subjectivities that live a precarious existence as a result of their race or ethnicity, their poverty or migration status, or even their disability. Used as a verb, 'to queer' means to resist, tweak, resignify and subvert expressions and acts of hatred, abuse, exploitation, discrimination and violence to those 'others' invented by dominant societies.

This form of 'being here' resists and surpasses not only dominant and exclusive categories, but also static and determining sex-gender paradigms. Beyond essentialist dichotomies such as man/woman, heterosexual/homosexual, queer theories come from socio-political movements that destabilise and neutralise the dualistic representation of these binaries that have been used as technologies for 'othering' people, whether in speech or action, and which have invented subordinate sensibilities, so creating areas of exclusion.[2]

Words signify and create language habits that leave marks on the body, so creating an infinite network of body semantics. When they are accompanied by hatred and violence and when they turn into words, physical actions that symbolise abuse, language habits produce deep wounds, marks of pain and rejection, sometimes incurable, on the savaged bodies. The slogan, 'We're here and we're queer,' as a public utterance, expresses a semiotics of hatred and exclusion, and raises a collective voice demanding that any queer body be treated with dignity. It is not a minor point that these protest marches had their high point during the time of the HIV and AIDS pandemic, when groups with impaired immunity, mainly homosexual and gender-diverse people who were being denied the necessary medical, psychological and spiritual attention, publicly resisted the labelling of their bodies as diseased and criminal. These 'AIDS-infected' bodies also formed part of a queer body, a fluid body, fighting together and caring for each other. We're here and we're queer! It's a slogan that calls for another world that is possible, still to come but appearing fleetingly in the present. Despite all the determinisms of the world and language, it is still possible to transform and give new meanings to our language habits and to build interpersonal relations that are based on mutual recognition, particularly by recognising the dignity of those bodies that live precarious lives in the diasporas of the world.

We're here and we're queer. Here, in the pilgrimage of a historical present yearning for a future that has yet to dawn, expressing an interpersonal desire to reach a different possible world. It is as though an *eschaton* (an end-state, a consummation, a plenitude), apparently unattainable, had paradoxically become incarnate – if only finitely and contingently – in that being here, in a fleeting present, but one imbued with a transforming and fulfilling meaning. Queer theory has its roots in these movements of social and political activism, social struggle and resistance that have carved out body semiotics able to open up breaches in walls, to burst into public, in anticipation of an extravagant eschatological celebration in which collective faith is expressed in a more liveable life, a living well for all, of all sexes and genders. By 'living well' we mean a set of social, economic, political, ecological, cultural and religious practices that promote the common good (including the well-being of the planet), rather than colonising and globalising, Eurocentric or neoliberal patterns of behaviour. Living well seeks the common good, not just in material terms but also affectively and spiritually, especially for those whose lives are on the edge.

Lives on the edge are not only the fate of LGBTTTI people who are rejected and made to suffer by hetero-patriarchal societies and religious groups. Queered bodies also include the bodies of women who have been repressed, raped or murdered. They are the bodies that have been victims of discrimination on grounds of race by societies that exclude people for the colour of their skin or their ethnicity. They are the bodies of indigenous individuals and communities who have lost their territories, the first peoples who have been systematically colonised by supremacist and rapacious ruling groups. They are the bodies of migrants who have been forced to abandon their original lands and who every day suffer abuse, exploitation, forced disappearance. They are the 'disabled' bodies that society tosses aside because they do not meet the standards for 'perfect' and productive bodies. They are bodies forced into poverty and hunger, rendered invisible. Queer bodies, wretched bodies. But here too it is possible to *queer* the body, to continue our collective resistance to emerge into our reality as a single body that shouts: 'We're here and we're queer. Get used to it!' For queer theory this implies being able to see a different world as possible, to imagine a different ontology, becoming a different, eschatological body that transcends, here and now, all the walls that divide us, and so bursts into the diasporas that tear open humanity and the planet.

The complexities in the meaning of *queer* as an inclusive, dynamic and eschatological body (that is, one constantly in the process of becoming) spark theological reflections that will be touched on here briefly and in a rather piecemeal way.

II How theology catches a glimpse of eschatology in the fluid present of a queer body

As a queer Catholic theologian, I regard theology as a pursuit that is not just theoretical but also about experience, critical as well as assertive, at once negative and positive, which draws on some doctrinal sources but also ventures into new grammars, semiologies and epistemologies through a process of learning and dialogue with ecumenical and inter-faith ideas, among others. I encourage a theology of dialogue that also pays attention to secular discourses that collectively seek what it means to live well, not only for the human *corpus*, but also for the ecological and planetary body. Here the-ology is understood as a logos, an inexhaustible knowledge, a perpetual tasting that stimulates the appetite for the inexhaustible desire of God, a desire to love even more, as God loved us from the beginning of creation and continues and will continue to love us after the end of the ages. Theology is an attempt at learning that stimulates the intellect but springs from the heart and the bowels. That is why it also implies an affective process, a conversion of heart that in particular learns to recognise and join in solidarity with wretched bodies. For the same reason I regard theology as an area of knowledge that is intrinsically queer, in that it comes into being through the call of the Other and creates a pleasant stirring of the heart and stimulates the appetite for sapiential discernment. Most particularly, queer theology explores different ways of learning to recognise where people are made invisible, wretched bodies, distorts the violent forms of domination that exclude and construct such linguistic and material diasporas, while also encouraging mutual assistance – especially care for bodies cast into the diaspora. I believe that queer theology must show itself in public and learn to say: 'I am here, we are here, fighting together, hand to hand, for a different possible world, for a different eschatology!' To make such an announcement possible it is necessary to queer the inner voice of theology, looking for accents that resemble the surprising sounds of divine love that particularly desires the bodies that are not desired, but labelled indecent because they resemble a love that, because it loves radically, subverts the order of the existing powers and overcomes the walls that divide us one from another. I suggest an exercise in theology that opens itself up to the excess of this divine mystery and transcendence but which, at the same time, affirms and positively intensifies material and bodily life and also brings to life the deeply immanent and situational sense of interpersonal relations and relations with the planet.

Queer theology is inexhaustible because there are always new frontiers to deconstruct, discover and explore. It not only yearns for a different possible world beyond the rigid, antagonistic and hierarchical dichotomies used to justify the exclusion of 'other' bodies, regarded as inferior and defective by the hetero-patriarchal technologies in power, but also wants them to be given the permanent right of residence in an intermediate space between human and divine agency. This in-between status, part of a process, both divine and human, shows eschatological traces in the nature and activity of queer theology. Eschatology is in fact central for queer theology: living the faith as the performative expression and practice of the coming into being of the other possible world, the break with and resistance to the frontiers that divide and antagonise us, the peace that subverts all hatred and violence, the eternal life in which life is not the full stop of the creation story – the consummation of the human and cosmic body in the radically loving embrace, a body participating infinitely in the perichoretic dance of the Triune God, the God who is *koinonia*, communion of love without end.

Christian eschatology, the doctrine of the last times, paradoxically implies a protology, a consideration of the beginnings, in such a way that the flow of the history of humanity and of the cosmos penetrates the spatio-temporal gaps between the Alpha point and the Omega point, between the beginning and the end of all creation. The beginning of creation expresses God's desire and freedom to create and share his love with the whole cosmos. The Alpha point of humanity and the cosmos is this principle of giving and love, the self-giving of God, who delights in a creative act that culminates in the *eschaton*, the end-times of all created things, the final barrier that separates us from others and from everything that breaks our connection with God. The book of Wisdom expresses this love God has for the things he has created:

> 'For you love all that exists,
> you loathe nothing you have made;
> if you had hated something you would not have made it'
> (Wis 11.24, New Revised Jerusalem Bible).

For LGBTTTI people and the whole myriad of despicable bodies, this is very important since often, especially in religious environments, they have been told that they were born with an intrinsic defect, disordered, indecent. For this reason, in the present life they are rejected and, in some places, tortured and murdered. By this same dominant logic, what lies in store for these queer bodies after death is nothing but eternal hell. But God queers this dominant logic, since he is immeasurable love and creates everything he creates in his act of giving a love so radical that it transfigures and resignifies all hatred and loathing of despicable bodies and shares his divine love without reserve.[3] At the beginning of creation there is this superabundant and delightful love that gives itself without reserve, and in the end-times, in the risen life, there will be the consummation of this radical love. The flow of time in the here and now is overflowing with this protology and eschatology that change he meaning of the 'present'. Past and future are spaces within the here and now and make it pregnant with the ineffable divine desire. While desire takes the name of 'eros', attraction and appetite for the other, love takes the name *agape*, unconditional and fulfilling love that gives itself to the other in a kenotic act. In God desire and love, though different from each other, are mutually complementary, since God's desire arrives simultaneously with God's love, which means that God's desire is composed of both *eros* and *agape*. If vital desire consists in wanting to be recognised, then God desires us first and last, and his recognition gives dignity to the undesirable, gives new meaning to those bodies that live precarious lives. In this sense, eschatology could very well be the queerest aspect of Christian theology.

Past, present and future participate in God's extravagant, queer love. God's desire for self-giving in love is shared even within the divine Trinitiarian community, through participation in a perichoretic dance of infinite love for the Other: to the extreme of excess of being-in-the-Other, being perpetually energised by a desire of common-union in diversity. The divine community is a loving relationship without subordination, unity in plurality; it is a co-eternal dance of giving and receiving, of a recognition of the other that overflows with love, an intensely intimate living together with the Other, in the Other and for the Other. The plurality and incomparable diversity of all creation is related to this radical dance of love. Therefore, by virtue of this same energy of love, God who is Father and Mother shares themself not only in the immanence of their Trinitarian and perichoretic *corpus*, but also within human pain and custom. Their love becomes more radical as they share their divinity, penetrating flesh and body, sharing their extravagant love flesh to flesh. That is why Jesus Christ is constantly queering and subverting the systems that exclude despised bodies; he recognises, includes and embraces the innocent victims of his time and of all history, past, present and future. His death on the cross also queers violence and proclaims a risen life in which death and hatred will cease to be the last word of human and creation history. His very body becomes queer when it becomes pregnant and gives birth to the *ecclesia*, the community of bodies that love each other beyond the frontiers of time and space. Moreover, the Holy Spirit is the queerest element of this Trinitarian love that gives itself, gifts itself. Neither man nor woman, neither animal nor thing, the Spirit of God freely loves all that it desires, spills over and transcends any boundary, fills us with an excessive and extravagant love that revitalises and reorients our desires towards a final destiny of eternal life and full union with God. The Holy Spirit empowers the powerless, promising a future that is still to come, but embodied in the diversity of gifts present in those bodies that are fighting for a more liveable life.[4]

Christian eschatology is called to decipher the pauses and beats of this dance that takes us into the corpus of Trinitarian love, into an infinite desire, already inherently queer.

III Queering despised bodies

'We were all baptised into one body...you are the body of Christ,' says St Paul (1 Cor 12.13,27). The unity of the body does not eliminate plurality or diversity; it integrates it, transfigures it and at the same time surpasses it by making it part of the one (divine-human) body of Christ. In Christ there are no differences that set us against each other or divide us. Our bodies have been queered and put on Christ like transvestites, in such a way that 'there is no longer Jew or Greek, there is no longer slave or free, there is no longer male and female; for all of you are one in Christ Jesus' (Gal 3.28). By virtue of this Christic body that participates in an infinite dance of the love of God-*koinonia*, our bodiliness, in a continual process, takes on a transitional ontology that journeys in pilgrimage towards the consummation of the end-time, when God and all creation will form a single body. For the world that rejects and nullifies the dignity and the agency of queer bodies, this Christic body that St Paul glimpses has to do with a body that is in solidarity with the 'unworthy', the most vulnerable, the dispossessed and deprived of the planet (1 Cor 12.23-26).

The divine *eros* and *agape* nourish this queer body, energising its constant growth. This nourishment compounded of *eros* and *agape* transitions towards its eschatological fulfilment, anticipating here and now the promised future of the banquet in God's love. At the end of the ages there will be the joy of the eternal banquet, a marriage ceremony that will unite creation with the 'lamb of God' (Rev 19.7), who offers his crucified and risen body as the bread of eternal life (cf Jn 6.35). The lamb is Christ, the innocent victim who opposes all violence and teaches us that at the eucharistic banquet it is possible to queer hatred by imagining and practising peace as performative acts of resistance, by living (partially and contingently), one day at a time, the promise that all crosses will disappear, and that all victims and excluded people will be special guests at this feast of love without borders. Human and divine desire feed off each other. The foretaste of this feast of eschatological love is shared in the eucharists of present, past and future history, transforming the guests into one queer body: a single body of solidarity, justice and mutual care. Consuming God, who as he enters our bodies makes us part of the body of Christ, must therefore include all bodies, especially those most wounded by a world that rejects them and sacrifices them violently as scapegoats. The words and actions of Jesus Christ anticipate this extravagant feast, because he himself invites to the table those whom society rejects and excludes. The purpose of the eucharist is to transform us into eucharistic beings and turn us into 'bread' to feed those who have the greatest hunger, physical, affective or spiritual.[5]

We need to decolonialise Christian eschatology and queer it of all its tendencies to plunder and colonise, its supremacist, Euro-centric, hetero-patriarchal and dominant tendencies. A task still to be started is to put in place processes of mutual feedback through a dialogue between Christian eschatology and other sacred eschatologies of first peoples and religious traditions beyond the borders of Christianised tropes. The eschatological insinuations of divine love as a queer desire, without borders or diasporas, allow us to assert the value of other forms of wisdom and other grammars that emerge from experiences, epistemologies and narratives in situations and hemispheres of diaspora. The final decolonialisation and queering of bodies is still to come. Nonetheless, in the spatio-temporal spaces in 'this' collective and migrant body resonate with the throbbing of the queer desire of God, who loves unconditionally and immeasurably, promising the delight and pleasure of an eternal feast of radical love.

Translated by Francis McDonagh

Notes

1. Throughout this article there will be an explanation of the different uses of the term 'queer', which can take on different meanings. The following texts have influenced this article to outline a queer theory and queer theology in relation to Latin American and Hispanic contexts: Marcella Althaus-Reid, *Indecent Theology: Theological Perversions in Sex, Theology and Politics*, London, 2000; David Córdoba, Javier Sáez y Paco Vidarte (ed.), *Teoría queer: políticas bolleras, maricas, trans, mestizas*, Barcelona, 2005; Brad Epps, 'Retos, riesgos, pautas y promesas de la teoría queer', *Revista Iberoamericana*, 74.225 (2008), 897–920; Diego Falconí Trávez, Santiago Castellanos y María Amelia Viteri (ed.), *Resentir lo queer en América Latina: diálogos desde/con el Sur*, Barcelona, 2013.
2. This article draws on various authors and texts, mainly from proponents of some queer theories and theologies. A key bibliography would be the following: Judith Butler, *Undoing Gender*, London and New York, 2004; *Bodies that matter: on the discursive limits of "sex"*, New York and London, 2011; Patrick S. Cheng, *Radical Love: An Introduction to Queer Theology*, New York: Seabury Books, 2011; Susannah Cornwall, *Controversies in Queer Theology*, Norwich, 2011; Gerard Loughlin (ed.), *Queer Theology: Rethinking the Western Body*, Oxford, 2012; Pablo Pérez Navarro, *Del texto al sexo: Judith Butler y la performatividad*, Barcelona, 2016; Patricia Soley-Beltran y Leticia Sabsay (ed.), *Judith Butler en disputa: Lecturas sobre la performatividad*, Barcelona, 2012.
3. For a position that is beyond all violence and resentment, see James Alison, *Faith Beyond Resentment: Fragments Catholic and Gay*, London and New York, 2001.
4. My main sources of inspiration in Trinitarian theology are the following: Hugo Córdoba Quero, 'Sexualizando la Trinidad: aportes desde una teología de la liberación queer a la comprensión del misterio divino', *Cuadernos de Teología*, 20 (2011), 53–70; Elizabeth A. Johnson, 'Trinity: Living God of Love', *Quest for the living God: mapping frontiers in the theology of God*, New York and London, 2011; Luis F. Ladaria, *La Trinidad, misterio de comunión*, Salamanca, 2005; John Milbank, 'Can a Gift Be Given? Prolegomena to a Future Trinitarian Metaphysics', *Modern Theology*, 11.1 (1995), 119–161.
5. The following texts have been the inspiration for this theology of the eucharist: Ángel F. Méndez Montoya, 'Eucharistic Imagination: A Queer Body-Politics', *Modern Theology*, 30.2 (2014), 326–339; *The Theology of Food: Eating and the Eucharist*, Chichester and Malden, MA, 2009.

Queer Liturgy

MARILÚ ROJAS SALAZAR

Performativity is one of the key elements in what we today call queer liturgies, in the sense of acts of inclusive subversion performed in sacred spaces where people have been excluded because of their sexual orientation, skin colour or economic status. It is relevant to highlight resentment in the sense of regaining feeling as an attitude that is counter-ideological, anti-system, anti-racist, anti-sexist and anti-elitist. It has become necessary to carry out a political and religious incorporation of eroticism into the liturgy in order to liberate it, since this space has been co-opted by the dominant discourse of power or terror at the diversity of races, sexualities, bodies, cultures and epistemologies that seem 'alien' to a world inhabiting a heteronormative system in the framework of Christian theology.

I Introduction

Bodies are prior to sign and symbolism varies with time, and therefore the Christian liturgy must reconstruct itself at its deepest symbolic meaning, because it has tamed the body, eroticism, pleasure and sensuality, and it needs to recover these elements in a dynamic flow if it is to respond to the realities of bodies that have been scattered into diasporas, despised: bodies excluded because of differences of sexuality, fragmented bodies, bodies subjected to violence, suffering bodies, bodies in desire, bodies in secret graves, impoverished bodies, bodies being trafficked, bodies that are offered for sale, bodies of throwaway women (feminicide) or women treated as refuse, bodies despised for their race, migrant bodies and the body of the despoiled earth.

Feminist theologians have opted for an alternative liturgical practice in which our bodies intertwine through dance, music, art, poetry and flowers as a performative act of resistance to traditional patriarchal and kyriocentric liturgies that tend to nullify bodies, eroticism, different sexualities and pleasure. Divine Wisdom or Ruah,[1] the name we prefer to give to the sacred experience, queers the androcentric and patriarchal language used to refer to God in the liturgy.[2]

'Expelling eroticism from the church, discarding it and throwing it into darkness and disgust, tore apart the heart of indigenous culture. By repressing indigenous sexuality, Catholic morality shook Mesoamerican cosmology to its foundations.'[3] And it was not just in Mesoamerica that this happened; in other cultures, too, disdain for sex, pleasure and bodily desire produced wounds in people and exiled them from religious institutions. One example is the LGBTTTIQ community, who in many places were denied participation in the banquet of inclusion (the eucharist), and the desire for communion was hurt so deeply as to produce painful resentment.

Nevertheless I propose the category of 'resentment' (regaining feeling) or feeling differently and positively, as does Diego Falconi Trávez,[4] because regaining feeling is the energy powering the possibilities of celebrating, healing and creating one's own spaces for celebrating life, even when our bodies have been subjected to violence, discrimination or exclusion simply because they are different, bodies that have been censored for not submitting to the heteronormativity of the dominant patriarchal systems that often prevailed in Church systems and liturgies. For those who think that contextual theologies, especially queer theology, emerge from the resentment of the colonised or are the product of past injuries, it is appropriate to posit re-sentment as a counter-ideological attitude that is anti-system, anti-racist, anti-sexist and anti-elitist. Regaining feeling implies thinking about the issues of sex, gender and desire, which do not just affect the LGBTTTIQ community, but everyone, since sexuality is the core of power relations. It follows that contributing to the thinking about creating and re-creating liturgies that transgress the dominant systems – like queer liturgies – are theo-politically necessary if we are to deconstruct the patriarchal systems. Regaining queer feeling is a necessary element to express the pain, the rage, the discomfort and the critical thinking about the colonisation of the bodies, sexualities and desires of the various people who have suffered one or more forms of exclusion on grounds of sexuality, ethnicity, skin colour or social class in a Christian environment.

II Performativity as a political practice of liturgy

When excluded bodies assemble in spaces different from traditional ones to express a desire for justice, equity and dignity in spaces where they can seek Christian liturgies, it is a political act. Judith Butler asserts that: 'One important argument... is that it matters that bodies assemble, and that the political meanings enacted by those assemblies are not only those that are written or vocalised.... In other words, forms of assembly already signify prior to, and apart from, any particular demands they make. Silent gatherings, including vigils and funerals, often signify in excess of any particular written or vocalised account of what they are about.'[5] These bodies use performative power to demand their inclusion, having been excluded from what are regarded as sacred spaces. While the infernal is understood as what is the same,[6] what is divergent, twisted, different or queer is the expression of divinity in the experience of a Trinitarian relational God composed of persons really diverse and united by love. When excluded people demonstrate as a sign of resistance, they make present the vulnerability of bodies that the dominant systems consider disposable or rubbish bodies. In this way vulnerability is the deeply symbolic strength to show oneself that resists domination, and not as vulnerability has traditionally been thought of, a synonym of weakness or fragility. Liturgy as a performative act can succeed in subverting the dominant discourse of power or terror (phobias) of the diversity of races, sexualities, bodies, cultures and epistemologies that are seen as 'alien' by a world that inhabits a universe that is heteronormative in outlook as part of Christian theology. It has to be understood that performativity consists in the repetition of actions marked by uses of language that place a regulatory ideal around the body, sex and desire, and so produce an imperative and power effects on people. This power effect is very often rigid and even one of exclusion and domination. Set within the Christian liturgy, these uses of language are opposed to the Gospel and in contradiction to it, and so set up figures to be despised.

If language produces effects, there is no body that is not at the same time a product of language and, in the case of homilies, sermons and reflections in the liturgy, we should ask ourselves: 'What language lies behind the bodies?' or, more accurately, 'What body lies behind this language?', because the language used produces what it describes and becomes a language of authority. What bodies are important for someone who raises one form of language as a banner, and what bodies are not important? If power is what shapes, upholds and regulates bodies, what power effects does homophobic, lesbophobic, racist, misogynistic or terror language have on the bodies that take part in a liturgical act? Or what power effects are there in a lovingly diverse language of incarnation, salvation and redemption implanted in bodies of diverse sexualities through gestures symbolising equity?

I recognise that every day in Latin America and the Caribbean more symbolic spaces are being created for alternative liturgies and their LGBTIQ members are in search of a Christian spirituality and practice expressed in liturgies full of shared music, colour, art dance and food, spaces for biblical and theological reflection that call for the recognition of the sexual, bodily, affective and spiritual dignity of the 'queer' people that take part in them. There is a deep desire for meeting and a longing for spiritual strengthening, for an intimate encounter with the divinity in these wounded and marginal bodies who have been denied their right to be at home in the house of the Father-Mother of Jesus of Nazareth. Liturgy as a performative act can bring about the subversion of this exclusion.

Some examples of queer liturgy are 'The queer theology café', a venue situated in the gay district of Mexico City where people of diverse sexuality and different Christian traditions meet to reflect on their faith. They share biblical texts using critical gender hermeneutics, they talk about the insights the text brings to their own life stories, many marked by painful experiences of exclusion from their churches. The group chats over cups of coffee and coffee smells and the odd dessert that helps to sweeten the lives of people sharing their vulnerabilities. On other occasions the group may take part in a public meeting or march in defence of the rights of the LGBTIQ community or put on a performance based on the characters of the text or experience they have discussed.

Another example is the 'CEBs small communities of women' (CEBs are Church base communities) that design their own liturgies around a biblical text with dances, floral crowns, prayers, incense, perfumes, fabric panels in bright colours symbolising the ancestral peoples, regional fruits and live music with the traditional instruments of each region. They tell the stories of the heroic actions of women of the bible and the experiences the women of the community have been through, the text may be dramatised (as a socio-drama), and they discuss the implications for the everyday lives of women and in the struggle for their rights or to defend their territories. Finally there are embraces and a sharing of food and drink.

One more example of queer liturgy is the Eucharistic celebration in Holy Family parish in Colonia Roma in Mexico City, which is organised by the Jesuits. It takes place every Sunday at 7.00pm. A group of diverse sex people take part in the liturgy with their voices, musical instruments and aspirations to be in the choir, and share the bread with the rest of the community. Sometimes a member of the group leads the reflection. In this space bodies from the diaspora unite in Eucharistic desire with the body of Jesus.

III The body, the feast of eucharistic desire

The bodies from the diaspora, especially those whose sexuality is different, become spaces of eucharistic desire, precisely because this table has been denied to them and they have been treated as the dogs that eat the crumbs that fall from their masters' tables (cf Mt 15.27). And the question arises: Who are the masters of this world? And who are those who are at the table distributing the bread of the world? Who are those who are feeding on the crumbs of society, what society has thrown away? Who are the despised of this world? Who are the vulnerable or those who resist this story of injustice? The body of Jesus, like a wounded body that resists domination and injustice, is also a body that is shared and forces us to rethink the experience of God outside the closet or Divine Wisdom, outside what is fixed, the boundaries fixed by culture, religion and traditional stereotypes, outside the walls and outside the heterosexual standardisation imposed by a society that insists on staying in the closet of phobias.

The bodies that are shared in the biblical texts are in the main those of women; these bodies are used to make peace deals, to acquire land, have the blessing of children and the fertility of the land. Women's bodies, in the past and still today, are good for commerce, to demonstrate economic power, political power, inherited title, to mark territory. Women's bodies are market commodities both in the ancient world and in the neoliberal world we live in today. That is why talking of Jesus' body as a body that is shared means linking it to the bodiliness of women and breaking with the male patriarchal stereotype. In our cultures it would seem that only the female body has to give itself, to surrender itself, to give everything... whereas the man's body is entitled to receive this gift and has the right to pleasure, to possession, the right to eroticism and the space need to live.

At every celebration of the eucharist we celebrate the memorial of the feast of the body and blood of Christ shared as food for humanity. It is a feast of the body and so a feast of flesh. It is in the flesh of our bodies that everything happens: history, love, everyday life, pain, suffering, yearnings, ideals, dreams, eroticism, sensuality, plans, choices. It is the feast of food and drink. Above all, it is the feast of the despised bodies that share themselves without worrying about the gender categories in which the rules place them. The body of Jesus becomes the table that awakens the Eucharistic desire for a life with dignity, equality and justice, and the desire to belong to a community that is inclusive, loving and desirous of a better quality of life for those who have been excluded by reason of race, sex or social condition. Jesus is a body that gives itself and also breaks down 'the closet' of the stereotypes of his time; he shows himself in a glorified body in which gender stereotypes are transcended (if not abolished), and into which despicable bodies are incorporated.

IV Erotic love as a force of fulfilment and resistance

Erotic love is a fundamental element of the body and I maintain that as an energy generating fulfilment and resistance it should be incorporated into the liturgy, from which it was exiled a long time ago, though despite the efforts to abolish it, it survived in the medieval mysticism of men and women in the history of Christianity and found its best setting precisely in the liturgy. Audre Lord suggests that erotic love should be thought of as a life-force, but we need to add that it is a source-force that enables us to resist or oppose violence.[7] From erotic love flows the ability to transgress oppressive and violent systems, the vitality to transform spaces of injustice into spaces of equity and relationship; it is also the ability to subject to critical analysis the forms of language that nullify the desires and passion that flow from our bodies and their yearning for different forms of a dignified life. Erotic love is also a call to live what is called in the Andes *suma kawsae*, understood as the right to live well or have a good life. Erotic love has a deeply political dimension that enables us to recognise acts of pornography as the selling of bodies, and it keeps its distance from pornography, identifying it as the daughter of the god Market. On the other hand, erotic love cannot be isolated from its relationship with Sophia because otherwise it would fall into the void of naivety or ignorance of how to direct its power, passion and desire. Sophia needs the relationship with bodily erotic love in a harmonious union of sensuality and pleasure because without this Sophia would be mutilated, since 'the relationship of those who come to Sophia seeking wisdom is entirely sensual and erotic'.[8] That is why I take the liberty of introducing *erosophia* as a category of knowledge drawing on the very ancient Hebrew concept of knowledge as a relationship of passionate love, intelligent, critical and bold, and able to lose all fear in the pleasure of recreating the relationships between all the species that inhabit this common home known as *oikos*.

This energy is not merely connected to bodies; it flows out of bodies as a spiritual force of resistance to the colonisation of what we have been calling erotic love. This force is interdependent because it is the ability of all living beings to relate to each other. The interdependence that is the mark of this force enables us to transcend the categories of domination, oppression and submission that belong to the colonial systems of domination with their hierarchical patriarchal structure.

Liturgy, then, finds expression in the space of erotic bodies from the diaspora, because erotic energy projects an individual towards a relationship with the Other, whereas narcissism places the subject in a degree of depression that prevents recognition of otherness. The queer-erotic liturgical action is the one that makes possible a relationship with otherness as an ability to recognise the emergence of subjectivities from the diaspora that come out of themselves through performativity.

V Symbols in queer liturgy

Language and discourse are the most important elements that make up the imaginary order of the symbolic, since they are the way, according to Jacques Lacan, that we materialise desires. The area of the symbolic is the recognition of Otherness so that it is not rendered invisible or nullified. Naming is the most subversive theological act possible because it is only God who names created things and makes them exist (Gen 1.1-31), though in Genesis 2.18-20 he shares his power with Adam. If the patriarchal order is maintained, it might be said that the power to name things is rooted in masculine forms, whereas it is not a power given to women, but that is not the focus of our thinking here; instead we are concerned with a shared power and the recognition of the power of otherness (diversity, difference, rarity, strangeness, what does not follow the norm). It is here that we break with the heteronormative patriarchal power of a God who centres his power in himself, as opposed to the image of Divine Wisdom or Ruah, which shares, accompanies, and comes out of itself to share its power of naming what has been nullified. Here we encounter the recognition of the diversity of creation, the fruit of the divine power that has not been named and which now demands a force of visibility based on the desire of God or the divinity to come out of itself in a 'queer' (odd or strange) act of sharing its power so that otherness may exist and be recognised. That is why the symbolic, the real and the imaginary are intertwined in the everyday life of LGBTIQ communities that practise a life of faith in the gospel of Jesus and express it in many different forms and symbols in the liturgy, though the 'queerest' aspect of the assembly gathered as a community of believers is precisely the alternative space that is created, where the hybrid nature of the symbols flows without being bound by a strict detailed set of rules or very often confined like the liturgy in communities that are more rigid and more concerned with the forms than with the liberating message that the liturgy can bring to inspire the participants.

The inclusion in queer communities of 'odd', 'strange' elements, or even some considered 'outlandish' in a more patriarchal, colonising and Eurocentric liturgy, contributes to a reconstruction and the incorporation of diverse cultural expressions, and so makes a reality of intercultural, interfaith, inter-epistemic and inter-relational dialogue. This is an act of subversion (changes the version) that is political in nature in which the liturgy is deprivatised, is brought into public space, claims a civic character insofar as it practises and defends human rights and gives visibility to bodies that are despised, excluded or treated as refuse by accepting them as members of the community of equals that Jesus wanted.

Translated by Francis McDonagh

Notes

1. In this article I shall use Divine Wisdom or Ruah as the name of God. Feminist theologians prefer to use these names so as not to continue referring to the divinity in masculine categories.
2. Here I use 'queer' as a synonym for hybridity, and not just to indicate LGBTIQ people.
3. Sylvia Marcos, *Tomado de los labios: género y eros en Mesoamérica*, Quito, 2011, p. 137.
4. Diego Falconi Trávez, Santiago Castellanos y María Amelia Viteri (ed.), *Resentir lo Queer en América Latina: Diálogos desde/con el sur*, Barcelona, 2014, p. 13.
5. Judith Butler, *Notes Toward a Performative Theory of Assembly*, Cambridge, MA, and London, 2015, pp 7-8.
6. Byung Chul Han, *La agonía del eros*, Barcelona: Herder, 2014, p. 6. English edition: *The Agony of Eros*, Cambridge, MA, 2017.
7. Audre Lorde, 'The Erotic as Power', *Sister Outsider*, Trumansburg, NY, 1984, and London, 2019, pp 53-59. Also available online: http://www.peacewithpurpose.org/uploads/8/2/1/6/8216786/audre_lorde_cool-beans.pdf
8. Susanne Schaup, *Sofía: Aspectos de lo divino femenino*, Barcelona,1999, p. 41. English translation: *Aspects of the Divine Feminine, Past and Present*, Lake Worth, FL, 1997.

A Queer (Beginning to the) Bible

GERALD O. WEST AND CHARLENE VAN DER WALT

Genesis is the starting point for an African queer biblical trajectory in this article. Locating queer African bodies as subjects of interpretation of the Bible, this article demonstrates how the book of Genesis has been used within actual African contexts to recognize a queer trajectory in scripture. The Bible, we argue, is a site of struggle, with contending trajectories/ voices, some of which are queer, particularly when read from LGBTIQA+ African social locations.

I Introduction

The Nigerian biblical scholar Justin Ukpong clarified and conceptualised the practice of African biblical scholarship when he argued that African bodies within African realities were 'the *subject* of interpretation of the Bible'.[1] Ken Stone makes a similar argument, identifying 'queer' 'as a kind of location in society',[2] and then going on to draw on the work of Mona West as a specific example of this kind of claim. West argues for queer social locations as the subject of interpretation of the Bible, insisting that biblical scholarship 'add the voice of the gay/lesbian/bisexual and transgendered community (Queers) to those marginalized groups who are reading the Bible from particular social locations'.[3] A queer social location is, however, not some vague conceptual notion but is concretely contextual and fundamentally embodied. In this sense, as both Stone and West implicitly acknowledge, African biblical scholarship and Queer biblical scholarship are sisterly sites of marginalization, reconstructed as the subject of interpretation of the Bible. Stone summarizes this understanding of Queer biblical interpretation as follows:

> 'a "queer reading of the Bible" is a reading produced by a reader who is "queer", where "queer" is understood to communicate lesbian, gay, or bisexual identities, experiences, or social locations; and where those identities, experiences, or social locations are thought to impact both the questions that one puts to the biblical texts and the answers one can imagine giving to those questions.'[4]

If the focus of this understanding of queer biblical interpretation is on the queer reader, Stone recognizes a second way of understanding queer biblical interpretation, where the focus is on the queer biblical text, 'on the fact that certain parts of the Bible itself can be read as "queer"'.[5] 'After all', continues Stone, 'coming as it does from that time prior to the emergence of modern systems of sex, gender, sexuality, and kinship, the Bible does not always cohere with heteronormative assumptions".[6] Queer biblical interpretation 'calls attention to unexpected configurations of sex, gender, and kinship in the Bible and its history of reception'.[7]

What South African queer biblical interpretation would add to Stone's formulation is the notion that the biblical text is itself, intrinsically, a site of contestation with respect to sex, gender, sexuality, and kinship. Given the recognition within biblical scholarship of redactional processes in which texts are regularly 'collected' and then 'composed', 're-collected', and 're-composed', Itumeleng Mosala identifies 'the question of "struggle" as a fundamental hermeneutical factor in the text, as indeed in the communities behind the text and those appropriating the text presently'.[8] While Mosala's emphasis is on class and gender as sites of struggle within biblical texts, we would add configurations of sex, gender, and kinship as sites of struggle within biblical texts.

Our contribution in this article is from an African queer perspective, limiting our analysis and reflection to actual biblical texts with which we have worked in African communities. African social locations, particularly African queer social locations, are the subject of our biblical interpretation. By foregrounding the interpretative practise of queer bodies in the African context in our reflection we aim to amplify the transgressive action made possible within a queer methodology and in the process, we deliberately ask serious questions about the power dynamics within the interpretation process. Rather than limit the impact of the biblical text to ecclesial and academic institutions to be overseen by designated clergy or teachers, we believe in the process of a queer taking back of the Word in order for more bodies to matter. Further, our contribution is limited to the beginning of the Bible, the book of Genesis, both because we want to engage with biblical text in some detail within the limited space of this article and because the reception of Genesis in African contexts provides theological shape to the Bible as a whole. In terms of African communities of Christian faith, the Bible's theological shape derives from Genesis, particularly when it comes to matters of sex, gender, sexuality, and kinship. A recognition of the queerness of Genesis points to the possibility that scripture as a whole might be queerer than we have imagined.

II The queer shape of the second creation story (Genesis 2)

In his book, *A question of truth: Christianity and homosexuality*, Gareth Moore deals not only with what he calls 'The Bible against homosexuality?', but also 'The Bible for heterosexuality?'. The question marks in each case are instructive, for Moore interrogates both the well-worn allegedly 'anti-homosexual' biblical texts and the familiar allegedly 'pro-heterosexual' ones. In dealing with Genesis 2, our focal text in this section, Moore counters the 'standard view' by qu(e)erying this view.[9]

Moore begins with a queer question. 'What, then', asks Moore, 'can we legitimately get out of the plain meaning of this text' (Genesis 2) for the purposes of an 'appropriate Christian attitude towards homosexual relationships'?[10] Moore is not a biblical scholar and is unaware, for example, of the pioneering narrative work of Phyllis Trible on Genesis 2 and the array of biblical scholarship that has clustered around Trible's analysis.[11] But he is a reasonably careful follower of the narrative (in English translation).

Moore's queer question discerns a queer shape in the narrative. The narrative shape of Genesis 2 in broad terms, following Aristotle and others,[12] includes an exposition in which God 'made' earth and the heavens (but incompletely, as the complications that follow indicate), a series of intersecting complications, and series of intersecting resolutions to those complications.

'7 And Yahweh God formed ha-adam [the earth-creature] (of) dust from ha-adamah [the earth] [...]

18 And Yahweh God said,
"It is not good for ha-adam to be alone;
I will make for it a companion corresponding to it".

19 And Yahweh God formed from ha-adamah
every beast of the field and every bird of the heavens
and brought each to ha-adam to see what it would call each one.

20 And whatever ha-adam called each living nephesh,
that was the name. [...]
But as for ha-adam, it did not find a companion corresponding to itself.

21 And Yahweh God caused a deep sleep to fall upon ha-adam
and, while it slept, took one of its ribs [...]

22 And Yahweh God built the rib
which Yahweh God took from ha-adam into woman (ishshah)
and brought her to ha-adam.

23 And ha-adam said:
This, finally, is bone of my bone
and flesh of my flesh.
This shall be called woman (ishshah)
because from man (ish) was taken this.'[13]

Trible's recognition of the androgynous identity of *ha-adam* is in itself the recognition of a crucially queer aspect of the text. The text plays with words, invoking a resonance between 'the earth' that God has made and the 'earth-creature' that God makes from 'the dust of the earth' (7). From this androgynous 'earth-creature' God later makes two sexed creatures, 'man' and 'woman'. (We find a similar implied process in Genesis 1.27, with 'male and female' created from *ha-adam*, though the process is not made explicit.)

Our focus, however, is on the particularly queer narrative shape of this unit. The focus on this unit resides in the complication that the creature God has made in verse 7 is acknowledged by God, using direct speech, to be 'alone', and that this is 'not good'. The way God goes about resolving this complication is profoundly queer. Briefly,[14] God's resolution to the complication is to make a companion for the earth-creature (18). What is queer is that God begins by forming animals, wondering if, perhaps, there may be among the animals an appropriate companion (19–20). What is even more queer is that God gives the earth-creature the right to make the choice (20). God does not dictate. The earth-creature is the agent of the act of recognition.

When the earth-creature does not find a suitable companion among the animals God has formed (20c), God follows another course of making. God now builds a companion from the very body of the earth-creature (22). God then brings the product to the earth-creature, as God brought the animals. The narrative shape is identical. What follows too is identical, in terms of narrative shape. The earth-creature again is the agent of recognition.

We pause here to allow this queer narrative shape to be recognized. God does not decide that this is now an appropriate companion. The earth-creature decides. The Christian tradition has tended to emphasise the product: a woman. A queer interpretation emphasises the process: that it is left to us to decide who our appropriate companion is.

The recognition and acceptance of an appropriate companion is a human responsibility. God creates and the human chooses. If we pause, as we might, at 23a (emphasizing the process), we might imagine a range of other human options that the earth-creature might recognize and accept as its companion. The full range of human companions and/as human sexualities is present in *ha-adam*. *Ha-adam* is inclusive of us all.

III Que(e)rying Genesis 19 with Genesis 18

The reception history of Genesis 19 in African contexts is unambiguous. Genesis 19 is about God's condemnation of homosexuality. The Ujamaa Centre for Community Development and Research, with which we both collaborate, began working with Genesis 19 as part of its work in the area of gender-based violence in the late 1990s. A landmark Contextual Bible Study (CBS)[15] on the story of the rape of Tamar in 1996 propelled the Ujamaa Centre into sustained work on various aspects of gender-based violence,[17] including the rape of men. We chose Genesis 19 because we hoped that using this biblical text would open up community space for more direct work on homosexuality. The logic of our choice of this text at the time was that by using this allegedly homophobic biblical text we might deconstruct homophobic receptions of Genesis 19, reading the text instead as a condemnation of (heterosexual) male rape.[17]

The advent of HIV generated more overt queer community space within which to engage aspects of sexuality, including homosexuality, more explicitly. This change in the South African context and increasing attention within biblical studies to homosexuality combined to offer access to details of the biblical narrative that had been neglected in our earlier CBS. Re-reading Genesis 19 within its literary-narrative context of Genesis 18 provided significant capacity for community-based conversation about 'homosexuality' by posing the question of whether Genesis 19 had anything at all to do with homosexuality. Genesis 18, so clearly a narrative about Abraham's rural hospitality to three strangers, provided the narrative frame for recognizing Genesis 19 as equally clearly the story of Lot's urban hospitality to two of these very same strangers.[18] Genesis 18–19 were a single narrative about hospitality, not homosexuality.

In a workshop in April 2013 with the Gay & Lesbian Network and clergy from the region we constructed a CBS on Genesis 18–19 that focused specifically on hospitality. Here our attention was less on how clergy appropriated this re-read biblical text than on the appropriations of self-identified lesbian, gay, and trans participants.[19] Their appropriations, reported here, were wonderfully queer: 'The church is like Sodom, just as the men of Sodom wanted to subject others to their power, so the church wants to subject us to its power. Re-reading this text reminds us to question each and every text; God himself will come down to judge the church, just as God himself came down to judge Sodom!' This theme was taken up by others, who asked, 'Could not this text, as it is interpreted by Ezekiel and Isaiah and Jesus, be read as a story about receiving and welcoming homosexuals into our churches?'[20]

Such remarks by African LGBTIQA+ interpreters encouraged us to continue to explore the possibility of further engaging with this particular story in order to continue troubling exclusivist and harmful Bible interpretation practises. At the 2017 Eudy Simelane Lecture[21] we were collectively taken aback when engaging with queer people of faith from rural KwaZulu-Natal in a CBS exercise when queer believers insisted that the Bible is indeed against queer love and that there is no conversation to be had on the matter with religious leaders or people of faith. We returned to Genesis 18, wondering whether the character and the positionality of Sarah in the Genesis 18 narrative might help us to consider notions of insider/outsider and subject/object in the text. By drawing on notions of hospitality and the possibility for encounter and recognition when strangers risk crossing boundaries to meet each other, we constructed a CBS that would help faith leaders to reconsider the gifts LGBTIQA+ might people bring to the community of faith, and that would help LGBTIQA+ people to shift from objects of discussion to embodied subjects,[22] like Sarah. The transformation in Sarah's positionality within this beautiful narrative of encounter has created space for conversations that will hopefully in time allow more bodies to matter.

IV A queer Joseph (Genesis 37)

As a brief last example from the book of Genesis we would like to reflect on the richly complex Joseph narrative cycle.[23] Joseph is a well-known and eagerly appropriated character in the African context, favourite son of the favourite wife, dreamer, slave, and finally imperial overlord.[24] It is precisely because of the resonances and contending interpretations that the Joseph narrative has become a rich pedagogical tool as we journey with our students though a slow narrative engagement.

Beyond the religio-cultural and socio-economic complexities raised by the narrative, we have found the work of the queer drama scholar Peterson Toscano exceptionally helpful in the process of intersecting religio-cultural and the socio-economic with gender and sexuality.[25] Toscano picks up on Joseph's gender non-conforming character in one of his performance lectures and we draw from this creative work in order to reflect on Joseph, the indoorsy and dreamy favourite son, as an example of a character who transgresses gender norms in the Bible and does not adhere to prescribed gender constructions or expectations. We try to set up a playful pedagogical engagement with the character of Joseph and appropriate off-beat references, ideas and terms embedded within the narrative in order to destabilize the norm and hopefully, in the process, crack open more space for creative conversations.

We will limit ourselves to three short examples here to illustrate something of the inherent queerness of the narrative. Firstly, the fact that Jacob gifts Joseph with a coat of many colours is probably remarkable in and of itself, but that this garment, which has the clear function of an identity marker, is described by the same word that is used to describe Tamar's dress, fit for a princess, in 2 Samuel 13 opens up an array of queer interpretative possibilities. Jacob gifts Joseph with a princess dress and in the process the outsider is colourfully othered. Secondly, Joseph's distinctly marked otherness, which is amplified by the princess dress, evokes punitive reaction from his brothers. They see him from afar and is affronted by his display of otherness as he comes to visit them in the field. Their physical disciplinary action to his queerness is reminiscent of similar 'corrective' behaviour expressed though the rape of lesbian woman in the African context who do not conform to the heteronormative ideal. This painful and dramatic moment in the Joseph narrative cycle often functions as a dynamic reflective surface that enables contextual discussions of punitive violence against queer bodies. Thirdly, and connected to the previous points, the counter-dominant construction of Joseph's masculinity in his tearful forgiveness of his brothers and his lack of sexual vigour with Potiphar's wife, makes him and ideal character to engage contemporary discussion on dominant notions of masculinity and related sexuality and gender identity discussions.

V Conclusion: A queer biblical trajectory

Genesis, we have argued, is a queer beginning to the Bible. We have chosen to focus on actual African engagements with particular parts of Genesis, neglecting many other queer features of the book of Genesis. But even this limited focus makes it clear that scripture offers us a queer trajectory. We can follow this trajectory, as a site of struggle, across the texts of scripture,[26] into the gospels,[27] where Jesus too inhabits queer textual contours, refusing to behave as a 'proper' man, celebrating eunuchs, and constructing 'fictive' kinship communities.

We offer these reflections not as final conclusions or as a 'how-to' guide for Bible engagement, but rather as part of a process to destabilize and trouble that which is considered normal or unquestionable when it comes to the Bible and the engagement of issues and bodies situated in the intersection of gender, sexuality, and religion in Africa. We offer these reflections in order to move beyond the stalemate that so often exists, and that finds expression in the dictum 'the Bible says it, I believe it, that settles it', and so hopefully to move to more creative and life affirming spaces for Bible engagement and reflection.

Notes

1. Justin S. Ukpong, 'Rereading the Bible with African Eyes', *Journal of Theology for Southern Africa*, 91 (1995), 5.
2. Ken Stone (ed.), *Queer Commentary and the Hebrew Bible*, Cleveland: The Pilgrim Press, 2001, p. 16.
3. Mona West, 'Reading the Bible as Queer Americans: Social Location and the Hebrew Scriptures', *Theology and Sexuality*, 10 (1999), 30. For further discussion on 'social location' see Fernando F. Segovia and Mary Ann Tolbert (eds.), *Reading from This Place: Social Location and Biblical Interpretation in Global Perspective*, Volume 2, Minneapolis: Fortress Press, 1995.
4. Stone, *Queer Commentary and the Hebrew Bible*, p. 19.
5. Ken Stone, 'Queer Criticism', in Steven L. McKenzie and John Kaltner (eds.), *New Meanings for Ancient Texts: Recent Approaches to Biblical Criticisms and Their Applications*, Louisville: Westminster John Knox Press, 2013, p. 163.
6. Stone, 'Queer Criticism', p. 163.
7. Stone, 'Queer Criticism', p. 163.
8. Itumeleng J. Mosala, *Biblical Hermeneutics and Black Theology in South Africa*, Grand Rapids: Eerdmans, 1989, p. 125.
9. Gareth Moore, *A Question of Truth: Christianity and Homosexuality*, London: Continuum, 2003, p. 134.
10. Moore, *A Question of Truth*, p. 139.
11. Phyllis Trible, *God and the Rhetoric of Sexuality*, Philadelphia: Fortress, 1978; Beverly J. Stratton, *Out of Eden: Reading, Rhetoric, and Ideology in Genesis 2–3*, Sheffield, England: Sheffield Academic Press, 1995.
12. Aristotle, *Poetics*, translated by Gerald F. Else, Ann Arbor: The University of Michigan Press, 1967, p. 30; David J. A. Clines, 'Reading Esther from Left to Right: Contemporary Strategies for Reading a Biblical Text', in David J. A. Clines (ed.), *On the Way to the Postmodern: Old Testament Essays, 1967-1998*, Sheffield: Sheffield Academic Press, 1998, p. 5; Jerome T. Walsh, *Old Testament Narrative: A Guide to Interpretation*, Louisville: Westminster John Knox Press, 2009, p. 14.
13. Our translations are based on Trible, *God and the Rhetoric of Sexuality*, pp. 75–115.
14. For a fuller analysis, see Gerald O. West, 'Deploying Indecent Literary and Socio-Historical Detail for Change: Genesis 2:18–24 as a Resource for Choice of Sexual Partner', in L. Juliana Claassens, Charlene van der Walt, and Funlola O. Olojede (eds.), *Teaching for Change: Essays on Pedagogy, Gender and Theology in Africa*, Stellenbosch: Sun Press, 2019, pp. 57–78.
15. Gerald O. West, 'Reading the Bible with the Marginalised: The Value/s of Contextual Bible Reading', *Stellenbosch Theological Journal 1.2* (2015), 235–261.
16. Gerald O. West and Phumzile Zondi-Mabizela, 'The Bible Story That Became a Campaign: The Tamar Campaign in South Africa (and Beyond)', *Ministerial Formation*,

103 (2004), 4–12.
17. Gerald O. West, 'Reconfiguring a Biblical Story (Genesis 19) in the Context of South African Discussions About Homosexuality', in Ezra Chitando and Adriaan van Klinken (eds.), *Christianity and Controversies over Homosexuality in Contemporary Africa*, Oxford: Routledge, 2016, pp. 186–188.
18. West, 'Reconfiguring a Biblical Story', pp. 188–193. For other queer detail in these texts see Stone, 'Queer Criticism', pp. 166–170.
19. West, 'Reconfiguring a Biblical Story', pp. 193–196.
20. West, 'Reconfiguring a Biblical Story', p. 196.
21. The South African woman's football star Eudy Simelane was raped and murdered in KwaThema in Gauteng, South Africa, because she was an openly queer person. South Africa is considered to be the birth place of so-called 'corrective rape', an act of violence against women committed by men ostensibly to 'cure' lesbians of their non-conforming sexual orientation, or 'correct' them for it, 'disciplining' them to be 'proper' heterosexual women. In an attempt to mainstream conversations pertaining to LGBTIQA+ people in African faith communities, since 2016 the Ujamaa Centre started hosting, with the support of her family, the annual memorial Eudy Simelane Lecture which aims to honour the legacy of Eudy Simelane. See also Gerald O. West, Charlene van der Walt, and Kapya J. Kaoma, *When Faith Does Violence: Re-imagining Engagement between Churches and LGBTI Groups on Homophobia in Africa*, Johannesburg: The Other Foundation, 2017.
22. See Miroslav Volf, *Exclusion & Embrace: A Theological Exploration of Identity, Otherness, and Reconciliation*, Nashville: Abingdon Press, 2010.
23. See also Theodore W Jennings, *Jacob's Wound: Homoerotic Narrative in the Literature of Ancient Israel*, London: A&C Black, 2005.
24. Gerald O. West, *The Stolen Bible: From Tool of Imperialism to African Icon*, Leiden and Pietermaritzburg: Brill and Cluster Publications, 2016, pp. 410–420.
25. For more on Toscano's work see https://petersontoscano.com/.
26. See Robert E. Goss and Mona West, *Take Back the Word: A Queer Reading of the Bible*, Cleveland: Pilgrim Press, 2000; Stone, Queer Commentary and the Hebrew Bible.
27. Theodore W Jennings, *The Man Jesus Loved: Homoerotic Narratives from the New Testament*, Cleveland: Pilgrim Press, 2003; Stephen D. Moore and Janice Capel Anderson (eds.), *New Testament Masculinities, Volume 45, Semeia Studies*, Atlanta: Society of Biblical Literature, 2003.

Queer Muslim Theologies

SHANON SHAH

This contribution uses a postcolonial perspective to outline the range of contemporary queer Muslim theologies. It highlights the multiple challenges that occur when gender and sexuality become fault-lines in ideological debates that presuppose a 'clash of civilisations' between Islam and the West. I focus on the consequences of this 'clash' paradigm on the emergence of queer Muslim theologies in different contexts, comparing and contrasting their main assumptions and approaches. Queer Muslim theologies thus provide a crucial lens to analyse the diverse contestations of power and politics within the contemporary landscape of Islam.

I Introduction

It is overwhelmingly assumed by many Muslims and non-Muslims that Islam can never accommodate lesbian, gay, bisexual or transgender (LGBT) equality or inclusion. This was, for example, the underlying message of the Muslim parents who participated in a controversial, protracted protest against the teaching of relationships and sex education (RSE) and LGBT equality at Anderton Park primary school in Birmingham, England, in 2019. According to protest leader Shakeel Afsar, 'All we are concerned [about] is we are having our children come home with material that contradicts our moral values.'[1] Yet this public confrontation between supposed custodians of Islam and pro-LGBT teachers has rendered numerous other people invisible, especially the Muslim parents who supported the school's curriculum, whose views are marginal and considered sinful or heretical by those Muslims who believe that Islam explicitly condemns same-sex relationships and transgender inclusion.[2] A recurring theme in this storyline is that Muslims need to oppose LGBT equality because it is being imposed on them as part of an imperialist 'Western' agenda.

What happens to people who identify as Muslim *and* L/G/B/T? How or why would they even try to reconcile their religious beliefs and their gendered or sexual predispositions, given the polarizing and toxic nature of the debate?

This article proposes a typology of the range of queer Muslim theologies from a postcolonial perspective. The first half explains the conceptual basis for this typology whilst the second half provides examples of each 'ideal type' in this repertoire of interpretations. I mainly draw on my doctoral research which compared the experiences of gay, bisexual and lesbian Muslims in Malaysia and Britain, involving participant observation, in-depth interviews, and media analysis between 2012 and 2013, supplemented by my continuing engagement with several of my participants in both countries. My research also engages with my personal experiences and reflections as a gay Muslim man who was born and raised in Malaysia and is now based in Britain.

Admittedly, 'queer' is not a term that many LGBT Muslims might adopt to describe themselves. In this article, I therefore adapt the approach of the queer theologian Linn Marie Tonstad, who distinguishes between 'apologetics for the inclusion of sexual and gender minorities' (which I refer to as 'LGBT-inclusive' interpretations, understandings or expressions of Islam) and 'queer theology' as a way of imagining a 'socio-political transformation' that alters 'practices of distinction harming gender and sexual minorities as well as many other minoritized populations'.[3] My usage of 'queer Muslim theologies' explores the parameters of this latter understanding of 'queer theology'.

It might further be argued that 'queer theology' is rooted in a Western, Christian context. Yet if many Muslims agree that Islam is a religion of 'social justice',[4] then it makes sense to discuss 'queer theology' which pays particular attention to how religious understandings relate to 'structures of oppression'.[5] Before exploring queer Muslim theologies, however, it is vital to contextualize the emergence of LGBT-inclusive understandings of Islam.

II Queer Muslims and the 'clash of civilizations'

Socially progressive Muslim movements in Muslim-majority and Muslim-minority contexts often incorporate LGBT-inclusive apologetics in their work, informed by the concept of 'multiple critique' introduced by feminist scholars.[6] Contestations of tyranny, injustice, patriarchy and heteronormativity within Muslim societies must thus be accompanied by a principled opposition to global inequalities that are rooted in Western political, economic and military dominance. From the standpoint of LGBT-inclusive Muslim understandings, this means that criticisms of homophobia, biphobia and transphobia within Islam must also be analytically integrated with opposition to racism and Islamophobia, especially in Western contexts.

This 'multiple critique' is imperative when discussing queer Muslim theologies because gender and sexuality are pivotal to the idea of a 'clash of civilizations' between the West and the Muslim world. For instance, European elites in the Victorian era regarded Muslims as deficient because they were perceived as sexually licentious, whilst Muslim societies are now condemned for being too repressive.[7] Such attitudes towards gender and sexuality are increasingly used to demarcate the boundaries between 'proper' Islam and the West. Even Far Right ideologues in the West are now selectively appropriating pro-feminist and pro-LGBT attitudes to inflame Islamophobic sentiments, a phenomenon that the sociologist Rogers Brubaker refers to as 'civilizationism'.[8]

For the gay Muslims I encountered in my research in Malaysia and Britain, this civilizationism often created what the sociologist W.E.B. DuBois referred to as 'double consciousness' – a sense of 'unreconciled [...] two-ness' which involves 'always looking at one's self through the eyes of others'.[9] The 'lived' or 'everyday religion'[10] of many of my participants instinctively and reflexively involved a multiple critique of Islamophobia, homophobia, biphobia and transphobia. The varying emphases in these multiple critiques depended on the country context – most significantly, whether Muslims form a majority or minority of the population.

In this article, I do not distinguish between the queer Muslim theologies expounded by 'experts' – including progressive academic scholars of Islam – and 'non-experts', or 'lay' Muslims. Queering Muslim theologies means exploring diverse sources and ranges of Islamic interpretations on gender and sexuality. I also use the term 'theology' loosely – often, what is being contested is not the nature of Muslim beliefs in the Divine, but the interpretation of specific Divine rulings in the worldly realm, or jurisprudence. Yet different approaches to Islamic jurisprudence often entail differing but unstated assumptions about the nature of God – the boundary between the theological and jurisprudential is often fuzzy. With this in mind, I now turn to a basic framework to discern the 'ideal types' in the range of contemporary queer Muslim theologies.

III A postcolonial typology of queer Muslim theologies

According to Rasiah Sugirtharajah,[11] the Bible has historically been used to uphold the colonial venture and its attendant logic as well as to resist colonialism. The exercise of power (and the lack of it) are central to Sugirtharajah's analysis, which makes it an especially relevant lens to analyse queer Muslim theologies.

Sugirtharajah[12] proposes six interpretive possibilities or 'readings' of 'how the Christian Bible fared in the experiences of both the colonizer and the colonized', each with its own set of assumptions and consequences – 'dissident', 'resistant', 'heritagist', 'nationalistic', 'liberationist', and 'dissentient'. Analysing the colonizer *and* the colonized is crucial because both positions are internally diverse and involve complex layers of opposition and obedience to the larger project of modern European colonialism. Yet opposition, obedience, or other possible responses often led to different consequences, depending on whether one was the colonizer or the colonized.

Dissident readings were early forms of 'oppositional discursive practice undertaken by some colonialists', for example, the Dominican missionary Bartolomé de Las Casas's (1487–1566) resistance towards Spain's treatment of native Americans.[13] *Resistant* readings were 'undertaken by the colonized, the very people who felt the heavy hand of colonialism, suffocating under its rapacity', such as Olaudah Equiano (1745–97), the freed West African slave who became an outspoken opponent of the slave trade.[14]

Heritagist readings are attempts by the colonized to 'retrieve cultural memory' from the erasure caused by the ideological components of European colonialism.[15] *Nationalistic* readings are those appropriated by the leadership elites of colonized nations after they gained territorial independence and were initially 'characterized by a mood of buoyancy and self-reliance' – they have often descended into authoritarianism and tyranny in several post-independence nation-states.[16] The post-independence developmental and political failures of many of these states gave rise to a strand of *liberationist* readings, exemplified by the emergence of liberation theology in Latin America.[17] Yet liberationist readings, for all their strengths, are often still Eurocentric. *Dissentient* readings are developed by those who have been doubly marginalized – by Western colonial powers and by their own post-independence, nationalist governments.[18]

Sugirtharajah's typology can be useful for analysing queer Muslim theologies with some adjustments, chiefly with queering the 'colonizer'/'colonized' dyad. The 'double-consciousness' and 'multiple critique' of many of the queer Muslims I encountered suggests that the colonizer-colonized relationship is neither binary nor static and can manifest differently in different situations. For example, in Malaysia, some of the gay Muslims I met felt colonized (still) as Muslims on a global level yet marginalized as gay people on a national level. At the same time, because they were classified by the state as Malay and Muslim, they carried ethnic, religious, and often class privileges within Malaysian society. Therefore, in the remainder of this article, I re-interpret Sugirtharajah's six-fold typology in the light of three core questions about queer Muslim theologies: are they undertaken by queer Muslims or heterosexual Muslims; do they primarily target Islamic teachings; or do they primarily target Western imperialism or neocolonialism?

IV The range of contemporary queer Muslim theologies
In this section, I draw upon findings from my own participant observation and in-depth interviews as well as other examples from the mass media to illustrate the variety of LGBT-inclusive interpretations of Islam and other queer Muslim theologies at work today.

a) Dissident readings
In parallel with Sugirtharajah, these are inclusive interpretations undertaken by heterosexual Muslim allies of LGBT Muslims that challenge patriarchal or heteronormative expressions of Islam. Examples include the public statements in support of LGBT inclusion by Marina

Mahathir, the Malaysian activist and former President of the Malaysian AIDS Foundation and current Board Member of the Muslim feminist organisation Sisters in Islam.[19]

The history and politics of such dissident readings mean that they carry different consequences in different contexts. For instance, Marina's dissidence was risky, since she began articulating it in the late 1990s, when her father, then (and current) Prime Minister, Mahathir Mohamad, had jailed his deputy premier, Anwar Ibrahim, on charges of corruption and sodomy. When dissident readings like these are carried out in Western contexts uncritically, they can amplify dominant stereotypes of Islam as exceptionally misogynistic and homophobic.

b) Resistant readings

These readings are based on similar premises as dissident readings but are carried out by LGBT Muslims. One pioneering example of this was the early work of the openly gay, Muslim-American scholar of Islam, Scott Siraj Al-Haqq Kugle. He[20] acknowledges the influence of Islamic feminism in his work, and systematically argues for LGBT-inclusive understandings of Islam on multiple levels – Qur'anic hermeneutics, the analysis of *hadith* (the recorded Traditions of the Prophet Muhammad), and *fiqh* (Islamic jurisprudence). According to Kugle, the Qur'an – which is the Revealed Word for Muslims – is silent on modern conceptions of 'homosexuality' and 'transgenderism'. He goes further to say that the Qur'anic world-view actually enjoins unconditional celebration of human diversity, but that this egalitarian ethos became distorted by the patriarchal, heteronormative political factions that emerged after the death of the Prophet Muhammad. This politicking influenced the interpretation of certain Traditions of the Prophet and even led to fabricated, homophobic hadith, which had a knock-on effect on *fiqh* rulings on gender and sexual relations.

While Kugle's work remains relevant and ground-breaking, it also largely functions as LGBT-inclusive apologetics rather than 'queer' or postcolonial theology. For example, he acknowledges that his approach is 'essentialist' – he regards gay, lesbian or transgender identities as innate and this presents him with particular analytical problems regarding bisexuality.[21] Meanwhile, as with dissident readings, resistant readings such as Kugle's have been criticised by postcolonial scholars and traditional Islamic authority figures as pandering to Western attempts to construct colonially compliant expressions of Islam.

c) Heritagist readings

In Malaysia, I came across recurring heritagist readings, exemplified by two of my participants unknown to each other – Amin,[22] a man in his mid-20s who was in a same-sex relationship but did not identify as 'gay', and Nonny, a woman in her late 30s who was also in a same-sex relationship and described herself as 'fluid'. Amin and Nonny both grew up in rural parts of Peninsula Malaysia – Amin in the north, Nonny in the south – and both said that they were aware in their childhoods of men and women around them who might be labelled 'gay' or 'trans' by English speakers. These individuals were a minority in their mostly Muslim villages, and their identities were never explicitly named, but they were included in village life in non-judgemental ways. These stories comforted and inspired people like Nonny and Amin, who knew they were 'different' as Muslims but also felt culturally distant from urbanized or Eurocentric forms of LGBT activism.

These stories resonate with the argument by the anthropologist Michael Peletz,[23] that there has historically been a high level of tolerance for 'gender pluralism' or 'heterogender homosexuality' in the Muslim Malay world. These heritagist readings can empower LGBT Muslims to reclaim their identities but they also run the risk of romanticizing, as opposed to queering, the past. In other words, Muslim societies have demonstrably been tolerant of sexual and gender diversity, but this tolerance was still predicated upon a hierarchy which privileged heterosexual relationships. Instead, contemporary LGBT rights activists claim full equality and inclusion as citizens of the nation-state, including rights to marriage, child-rearing, political leadership, and economic opportunities. Heritagist readings are therefore useful insofar as they distinguish between historical expressions of Muslim tolerance and contemporary struggles for equality in different political contexts.

d) Nationalistic readings

These readings often overlap with postcolonial and traditionalist Islamic criticisms of LGBT-inclusive interpretations of Islam. A strong version of the postcolonial thesis argues that LGBT activism is inherently imperialist because it imposes Eurocentric concepts of sexuality and diversity on non-

Western peoples.[24] Whilst some proponents of this thesis are primarily concerned with challenging Islamophobic strands in pro-LGBT Western activism, the argument has been selectively amplified by more traditionalist Islamic scholars who seek to discredit the work of scholar-activists like Kugle.[25] Such arguments can then be weaponized by nationalist elites in many post-independence Muslim states, supposedly on the grounds of resisting Western hegemony.[26] It is crucial to remember, however, that these readings are not solely produced by traditionalist heterosexual Muslims. For example, some of my Malaysian participants who identified more strongly with the Malay-Muslim status quo were quick to defend the country's anti-LGBT laws to preserve their own privacy, personal safety, and social privileges.

e) Liberationist readings
In the UK, groups such as Imaan, the London-based LGBT Muslim group founded in the late 1990s, are inspired by the work of scholar-activists such as Kugle. Newer collectives have emerged, too, promoting liberationist readings of Islam in relation to gender and sexuality, including Hidayah, a splinter group from Imaan, and the Inclusive Mosque Initiative, which does not solely focus on LGBT inclusion.

Encouraged by Kugle's work and influenced by their subjective positions as Muslims in the West, the activists in these groups engage in a multiple critique of sexism, homophobia, biphobia and transphobia within Muslim communities, and racism and Islamophobia in wider British society. However, their circumstances mean that they sometimes interpret the gender and sexual politics in Muslim-majority contexts from Eurocentric, albeit Muslim-minority, perspectives. This has partly led some postcolonial critics to dismiss them as 'Westernised elites' and the equivalent of 'native informers' of Western neo-colonialism.[27] Such condemnations discredit the many valid, evidence-based criticisms that these groups have of patriarchal and heteronormative Muslim communities within the West as well as their valuable interventions in debates about racism and Islamophobia.

f) Dissentient readings
At the time of writing, dissentient queer Muslim theologies within Muslim-majority countries are still inchoate and largely invisible.

However, throughout my research in Malaysia, I encountered sentiments by gay Muslims that qualify as dissentient readings. Instead of organizing as visible LGBT Muslim collectives, however, these gay Muslims I met preferred to integrate their LGBT-inclusive understandings of Islam into broader forms of activism for human rights and democratic reforms in Malaysia. Fauziah, a bisexual woman and observant Muslim in her mid-30s, expressed her rationale succinctly:

> 'Homosexuality is not a Western import, but rights movements are a Western import. And with the gay rights movement, sometimes I feel like we are importing things lock, stock and barrel, and don't take into account that traditionally or culturally, psychologically, we do things differently here. Maybe being so in-your-face works against us sometimes.'

g) Status quo readings

Where does this leave the example that opened this article? The Birmingham protesters appeared to advocate a strong version of the nationalistic reading explained above. But what about the Muslim parents who were secretly or silently uncomfortable with these protests? I would speculate that they disagreed with the protesters' aggressiveness but might have still agreed that same-sex relationships are sinful. Unlike the protesters, however, they might distinguish this *religious* conviction from the need to respect *civil* provisions for equality and non-discrimination. I would further speculate that this is the default position of most Muslims in the West and even in Muslim-majority countries – they are not actively or aggressively anti-LGBT, but they are content with the status quo of Islamic teachings on gender and sexuality. It is beyond the scope of this article to analyse the contours of this position or the specific reasons for it.

V Conclusion: Queer Muslim theologies, politics, and power

LGBT-inclusive interpretations of Islam are likely to remain marginalized and controversial as long as gender and sexuality fuel the polemics that postulate a 'clash of civilizations' between Islam and the West. This article has instead proposed a typology of 'queer Muslim theologies' from a postcolonial perspective. This has yielded examples of multiple critiques of the 'clash' thesis, focusing upon the 'double consciousness' of LGBT

Muslims in differing contexts and the sympathies of their heterosexual Muslim allies. The typology I have suggested, however, should not be taken as static or prescriptive; it is a heuristic tool to discern the assumptions and repercussions of existing queer Muslim theologies. If anything, this proposed typology reminds us of the diversity of Muslim interpretations of several issues, including gender and sexuality, and of the inseparability between theology, politics, and power.

Notes

1. BBC, 'LGBT Lessons Protests Spreading', BBC News, 16 May 2019, at https://www.bbc.com/news/uk-england-48294017.
2. Donna Ferguson, '"We Can't Give in": The Birmingham School on the Frontline of Anti-LGBT Protests', *The Guardian*, 26 May 2019, at https://www.theguardian.com/uk-news/2019/may/26/birmingham-anderton-park-primary-muslim-protests-lgbt-teaching-rights.
3. Linn Marie Tonstad, *Queer Theology: Beyond Apologetics*, Eugene: Cascade Books, 2018, p. 3.
4. John Esposito, *Islam: The Straight Path*, Oxford: Oxford University Press, 1988, pp. 33–34.
5. Colby Dickinson and Meghan Toomey, 'The Continuing Relevance of "Queer" Theology for the Rest of the Field', *Theology & Sexuality*, 23.1–2 (2017), 2.
6. Omid Safi, 'Introduction: The Times They Are A-Changin' – A Muslim Quest of Justice, Gender, Equality, and Pluralism', in Omid Safi (ed.), *Progressive Muslims: On Justice, Gender, and Pluralism*, Oxford: Oneworld, 2003, pp. 2–5.
8. Rogers Brubaker, 'Between Nationalism and Civilizationism: The European Populist Moment in Comparative Perspective', *Ethnic and Racial Studies*, 40.8 (2017), 1203.
9. W.E.B. DuBois, *Of the Dawn of Freedom*, London: Penguin, 2009, pp. 3–4.
10. Nancy T. Ammerman, 'Introduction: Observing Modern Religious Lives', in Nancy T. Ammerman (ed.), *Everyday Religion: Observing Modern Religious Lives*, Oxford: Oxford University Press, 2007, pp. 3–18; Meredith B. McGuire, *Lived Religion: Faith and Practice in Everyday Life*, Oxford: Oxford University Press, 2008.
11. Rasiah S. Sugirtharajah, *Postcolonial Criticism and Biblical Interpretation*, Oxford: Oxford University Press, 2002.
12. Sugirtharajah, *Postcolonial Criticism and Biblical Interpretation*, p. 44.
13. Sugirtharajah, *Postcolonial Criticism and Biblical Interpretation*, pp. 44–45.
14. Sugirtharajah, *Postcolonial Criticism and Biblical Interpretation*, p. 52–53.
15. Sugirtharajah, *Postcolonial Criticism and Biblical Interpretation*, p. 55.
16. Sugirtharajah, *Postcolonial Criticism and Biblical Interpretation*, p. 63.
17. Sugirtharajah, *Postcolonial Criticism and Biblical Interpretation*, pp. 65–66.
18. Sugirtharajah, *Postcolonial Criticism and Biblical Interpretation*, p. 67.
19. Shanon Shah, 'Liberal, Muslim, Feminist, and Comfortable', in The Nut Graph (ed.), *Found in Malaysia*, Petaling Jaya: ZI Publications, 2010, p. 204.
20. Scott Siraj Al-Haqq Kugle, 'Sexuality, Diversity and Ethics in the Agenda of Progressive Muslims', in Omid Safi (ed.), *Progressive Muslims: On Justice, Gender, and Pluralism*,

Oxford: Oneworld, 2003, p. 194; Scott Siraj Al-Haqq Kugle, *Homosexuality in Islam: Critical Reflection on Gay, Lesbian, and Transgender Muslims*, Oxford: Oneworld, 2010.
21. Kugle, *Homosexuality in Islam*, pp. 9–12.
22. I use pseudonyms for all my participants.
23. Michael G. Peletz, 'Gender Pluralism: Muslim Southeast Asia since Early Modern Times', *Social Research*, 78.2 (2011), 656–86.
24. Massad, *Desiring Arabs*, pp. 173–74.
25. Ovamir Anjum, 'Editorial: Elements of a Prophetic Voice of Dissent and Engagement', *American Journal of Islamic Social Sciences*, 34.3 (2017), v–xxii; Jonathan A. C. Brown, 'A Pre-Modern Defense of the Hadiths on Sodomy: An Annotated Translation and Analysis of Al-Suyuti's Attaining the Hoped-for in Service of the Messenger (S)', *American Journal of Islamic Social Sciences*, 34.3 (2017), 1–44; Mobeen Vaid, 'Can Islam Accommodate Homosexual Acts? Quranic Revisionism and the Case of Scott Kugle', *Muslim Matters* (blog), 11 July 2016, at http://muslimmatters.org/2016/07/11/can-islam-accommodate-homosexual-acts-quranic-revisionism-and-the-case-of-scott-kugle/.
26. Han Sean Ong, 'Najib: "Human Rights-Ism" Goes against Muslim Values', *The Star Online*, 13 May 2014, at http://www.thestar.com.my/News/Nation/2014/05/13/Najib-human-rightsism-against-muslim-values/.
27. Massad, *Desiring Arabs*, pp. 173–74.

Part Four Theological Forum

Exiles in the Global Village and Political Compassion

CONRADO ZEPEDA MIRAMONTES SJ

This contribution describes the pastoral work being developed by Christian-inspired civil associations with migrants in the region of Mexico and Central America, whose forced migration into exile is part of a global phenomenon. The pastoral work is seen as carrying out the mission to proclaim the Gospel in terms of political compassion to the most vulnerable people, who are living in situations of extreme violence.

I Introduction

Exile is always painful. Abruptly changing your whole life is very hard: leaving suddenly when you have not planned it; leaving your home country where you grew up and leaving the group of friends and relations where you feel you belong; leaving behind the customs and culture which are part of your identity. It is traumatic to be forced into exile: it has not been a free choice, you are rejected in the places you travel through and not welcome in the land where you arrive.

The dramatic upheaval suffered today by millions of migrants and refugees throughout the world has social causes such as hunger, war, violence, corruption and the grave consequences of climate change. Today it is estimated that there are more than 250 million migrants in the world, a conservative estimate which represents 3% of the world population. These people are far from home, living in a real exile that repeats the uncertainty and pain experienced by the people of Israel.

In Mexico we are witnessing the exile of millions of our compatriots who have left home in recent decades for the USA and Canada, to seek what their own country does not offer them. In particular, as churches we accompany the massive exile of Central Americans fleeing from hunger and violence. Since the end of 2018, this situation has worsened with the addition of caravans of thousands of people – families with women, old folk and children – as well as the regular flow of those who cross the frontier every year. These caravans have been organised with the aim of travelling through Mexican territory at the least possible risk, since it is on the migration route that the greatest number of crimes against them are committed. Mexico is the second greatest corridor of migrants in the world, and one of the most dangerous, with nearly 500 thousand migrants crossing our territory per year, without documents, suffering endless harassment, such as mutilation from travelling in freight trains, rape, theft, extortion and persecution. We have heard thousands of testimonies from migrants and refugees telling stories of ill treatment on their journey, their via crucis, but also stories of hope.

The stories of women migrants offer an example of these daily crucifixions: 80% of those coming from the Northern triangle of Central America who travel through Mexican territory take contraceptive pills, because they know that on their journey someone will probably take advantage of their vulnerable situation and try to 'hook' them to be trafficked, or they may be raped by public officials or organised criminals, some who even kidnap, rape or abuse them repeatedly.

Cecilia's story is typical of this systematic violence. She had been migrating for three months from her native Guatemala to the USA. She wanted to be a soldier in her own country, but because she was a woman, she had to offer the 'sexual services' demanded by her immediate superiors, which is why she left the army. Then she set up her own shop selling cosmetics. But a member of one of the gangs ('maras') began to pressurise her, charging her a 'floor rent' to be able to continue with her shop. She kept her shop going, but one day she did not have the money to pay the extorted 'rent', her debts mounted and she was threatened with death. Immediately, Cecilia fled her country to seek a better life and escape the violent gangs. I met her personally when she arrived at the Bojay shelter, in the state of Hidalago, near Mexico City. Cecilia came to talk and seek protection. On her journey through Mexican territory she had suffered two rapes, the first while she was crossing a lonely area with other migrants in the Mexican state of Chiapas on the frontier with

Guatemala. Hooded figures stole all their belongings and the women were raped by this criminal group. After that traumatic experience, she decided to seek protection from another migrant and became his girlfriend. In the middle of the journey, one night her migrant boyfriend decided to rob all her belongings and rape her savagely, leaving her abandoned along the way. This was the second time that had happened to her. Cecilia decided to join another group of migrants, which included a family, and she came together with them to the shelter where I was. She arrived terrified and asking for protection, because now the man leading the group was trying to abuse her. Cecilia could not stand it anymore. She was given protection and at present she is in the process of seeking asylum in Mexico.

II Political compassion

We in the churches who are accompanying these exiles believe that God is not indifferent to this painful situation. We believe that the God of Israel and of Jesus feels compassion and moves the hearts of believers to act in his name and put gospel compassion into practice. In migrants and refugees we have learnt to see the Crucified Christ, also with hope amidst their sufferings.

Sometimes political compassion leads the churches and civil society accompanying migrants to breaks the laws, when they are unjust, as in some states of the American Union where humanitarian aid is classed as a federal crime. The government of that country wants to discourage civil society and the churches from helping migrants and those who may be seeking refuge. These church and civil society groups organise the provision of water and food for migrants in the desert regions on their journey. They take them to hospitals to be cured of their diseases. They do this because they believe that we human beings have the right to travel freely; we all have the right to seek new economic, political and educational opportunities which have been denied us in our place of origin. So the churches defend the right to a roof, bread and a decent living. They are inspired by a belief in service to migrants as an expression of the love of God.

But evangelical compassion must not be naïve. It needs to contain a strong dose of respect for fundamental political rights belonging to all human beings in the public area. *Politikos* means the area of life in common, the good ordering of the city and the affairs of those who are members of it. Migrants and refugees are also a constituent part of the *polis*, as citizens in transit seeking somewhere where their human condition is respected.

From the gospel viewpoint, compassion cannot be detached from civic affairs, as if these were two separate entities. Compassion must be political so that it does not lose its power to change things. Being involved in other people's suffering and pain, as well as in their joy and hope, inspires actions promoting respect for the human rights of everyone and all communities. Thus *political compassion* links the gospel with practical action to respect rights that have been denied, among others: security, life, food, education, freedom to travel, work, home, since we all have the right to enjoy these basic requirements for human fulfilment.

This article describes how we have learned to reflect, in the light of the Spirit of God, on the stories of migrants and refugees with some of the terrible things they have suffered. We also want to record the experiences of the churches who look after migrants with gospel compassion. That compassion is not naïve but political. It means trying to help empower migrants as persons, to defend their human rights. In the light of the gospel, we have learnt to support life-giving processes, which are what God wants for humanity.

III By way of conclusion

Because of their extreme vulnerability, migrants and refugees are the first recipients of divine compassion and the churches' commitment. That is an essential characteristic of witness to the divine compassion that 'unnails the crucified'. But this compassion cannot be naïve; it needs to be active in defence of human rights. It translates into respect for the fundamental rights of every human being, especially those who have been denied them through their extreme vulnerability as members of population groups forced to migrate. Most of them are clandestine and enter different countries without official documents.

Political compassion is thus a current feature of the churches who accompany the exodus of people forced to migrate in the globalised world. With this compassion we act to transform accounts of death into stories of life. Such an experience is an anticipation of that full life we yearn for as a human and divine gift. That full life begins with the recognition of the rights of all those who live in a situation of extreme vulnerability, especially migrants and refugees who are the first intended recipients of redemption.

Translated by Dinah Livingstone

The Imperative of Reforestation in Fighting Climate Change in Asia

REYNALDO D. RALUTO

This paper focuses on the intimate connection between climate change and deforestation in Asia. It views reforestation both as a means to mitigate climate change and as reparation for ecological sins. It proposes that regenerating native tree species mitigates climate change and serves as an appropriate restitution for the ecological damages brought about by the colonization of our natural forests.

I Introduction

Scientists argue that we are presently experiencing a disturbing change in the climatic system due to the abnormal build up of greenhouse gases (GHGs) in the atmosphere which traps the heat and makes the earth dangerously warm. Although scientists became aware of the greenhouse effect in 1896, the first scientifically well-founded models date from the 1970s. In 1988, the World Meteorological Organization (WMO) and United Nations Environment Programme (UNEP) established the Intergovernmental Panel on Climate Change (IPCC) to provide assessments of the scientific basis, impact and future risks of climate change.[1] In 1990, IPCC affirmed the scientific evidence that 'greenhouse gas emissions lead to climate change'.[2]

II Two major contributors of anthropogenic GHGs in the atmosphere

There are two competing explanations of the abnormally increasing build-up of GHGs in the atmosphere. Some say that it is caused by natural factors such as volcanic activity, variations in the earth's orbit and axis, or the solar cycle. Others argue that it is anthropogenic or the result of human activities since the advent of western industrialization in 1750 that relies on fossil fuels and other non-renewable energy sources. In their assessment, the IPCC scientists concluded that it is *extremely likely* (95% certain) that climate change is 'caused by the anthropogenic increase in greenhouse gas concentrations'.[3]

Recently, unsustainable deforestation has been identified as another major contributor to the increasing anthropogenic GHGs in the atmosphere. When trees are burned or rot, they release the stored carbon dioxide (CO_2) back into the air. Moreover, forests and vegetation are considered 'live actors' in the planet and have a 'buffering effect' on climate.[4] Together with the atmosphere and oceans, they serve as an important planetary sink of CO_2 and other GHGs. Thus, fewer forests and less vegetation could mean a hotter planet.

III Deforestation in Asia as an urgent ecological concern

Without neglecting the fact that many Asian countries have made a distinct contribution to climate change due to their reliance on fossil fuels and other non-renewable energy sources, this paper highlights the alarming disappearance of forests in Asia as a more urgent ecological concern. Around the year 1500, the estimated forest cover of Southeast Asia was about 90% of its land area, of which less than half remains in 2004.[5] In some countries like Cambodia, the Philippines or Vietnam, old-growth forests have nearly vanished.[6]

Analysts show that the major causes of deforestation in Asia are due to unsustainable land use, such as the conversion of land to agricultural use.[7] This unsustainable approach was initially introduced by the Europeans who came in large numbers to Southeast Asia between 1500 and 1900[8] to colonize not only the people but also natural resources, especially forests. In the Philippines, for instance, the European colonizers promoted large-scale monocrop plantations of invasive alien species that replaced the indigenous species of the country. Indeed, this is a *colonization* of nature in the ecological sense of making the foreign species dominant. The systematic deforestation in Asia was dramatically worsened by the advent of western agrarian capitalism in the 19th century when 'large tracts of climax forest were cut to make way for plantations'[9] in the name of development.

IV Destroying the natural forests as ecological sin

As a focal ecosystem, the destroyed natural forests negatively affect almost all other ecosystems. Nevertheless, this is not the main reason why Christians need to be concerned with deforestation. From a theological perspective, it is *ecologically* sinful for human beings to destroy the community of life and the integrity of creation. *Laudato Si'* teaches that it is *sinful* to destroy the biological diversity of God's creation, to degrade the integrity of the earth by causing changes in its climate, to strip the earth of its natural forests or destroy its wetlands, and to contaminate the earth's waters, land, air, and life.[10] The consequences of ecological sin are complex as it destroys our relationship with God, neighbours, the Earth and with present and future generations.[11]

Laudato Si' calls us to hear the 'cry of the Earth' without neglecting the poor who are most vulnerable to the impact of climate change as they 'live in areas particularly affected by phenomena related to warming, and [whose] means of subsistence are largely dependent on natural reserves and ecosystemic services such as agriculture, fishing and forestry'.[12] Expectedly, other living species of the planet 'will not be able to adapt quickly enough to the changes and will simply become extinct'.[13] The destruction of their habitat due to massive deforestation means the loss of biodiversity.

V The imperative of ecological restitution

We have inherited an abnormally warming planet due to the past generations that not only relied on fossil fuels but also exploited the forests. As we leave this planet to the next generations, it would be a violation of the principle of solidarity and inter-generational justice if we bequeath to them an uninhabitable planet.[14] How will their right to a healthy environment be protected? Some authors suggest that if the perpetrators are still alive and capable, they are obliged to give justice to their victims and should equitably shoulder the cost of adaptation measures to slow or prevent climate change.[15]

The sacrament of penance offers a helpful framework that includes confession of sins, conversion of the sinner, and restitution of the damages of sins. Jürgen Moltmann argues that repentant sinners must do their best 'to eliminate the damage they have caused'.[16] In the context of deforestation, the main purpose of ecological reparation is not to let the forest recover itself so that we can resume plundering it again but to allow the Earth to reproduce and regenerate itself.[17] This living planet has 'the right to regenerate its bio-capacity and to continue its vital cycles and processes free from human disruptions'.[18] James LaFrankie advocated to 'rebuild our forests from native species' because they have 'a relationship to the land, water and other organisms that has developed over a million years'.[19] In the face of climate change, regenerating the native tree species can be an efficient mitigating measure and an appropriate restitution for the ecological damages brought about by the colonization of our natural forests.

VI Reforestation as reparation for ecological sins

Many Asian countries have opted to fight climate change through reforestation activities. In July 2017, about 1.5 million volunteers from the central Indian state of Madhya Pradesh planted more than 66 million tree species along the Narmada river in just twelve hours.[20] Since 2012, the Philippines has legally required all its able-bodied citizens over twelve years of age 'to plant one tree every year'.[21] Some ecologically conscious parishes in the country also require the faithful to plant a certain number of trees before receiving the sacraments of baptism and marriage.

Reforestation activities should be viewed both as a means to mitigate climate change *and* as reparation for ecological sins. This entails enriching the prevailing meaning of reparation for our sins to include the ecological damages we have done to nature. Thus, the ministers of the sacrament of confession should give a penance that is appropriate for the sins committed. For instance, they may ask the penitents to plant trees rather than simply pray the Lord's Prayer three times as penance for destroying the forest. They may also use the Season of Creation (September 1 to October 4) as the most appropriate moment to ritualize the community's ecological repentance through reforestation activities. In any case, reforestation advocacy should go beyond legal requirements.

Notes

1. *IPCC Factsheet: What Is the IPCC?* at http://www.ipcc.ch/news_and_events/docs/factsheets/FS_what_ipcc.pdf.
2. Cited in Dominic Roser and Christian Seidel, Climate Justice: An Introduction. Translated by Ciaran Cronin, London and New York: Routledge, 2017, p. 125.
3. Intergovernmental Panel on Climate Change, *Climate Change 2013 – The Physical Science Basis: Working Group I Contribution to the Fifth Assessment Report of the Intergovernmental Panel on Climate Change*, Cambridge: Cambridge University Press, 2014, pp. 12–13.
4. See James Lovelock, *The Revenge of Gaia: Why the Earth is Fighting Back – and How We can Still Save Humanity*, London: Penguin Books, 2007, pp. 63–64.
5. Navjot Sodhi et al., 'Southeast Asian Biodiversity: An Impending Disaster', *Trends in Ecology and Evolution*, 19.12 (2004), 656.
6. William Laurance, 'Forest Destruction in Tropical Asia', *Current Science*, 93.11 (2007), 1548.
7. Sodhi et al., 'Southeast Asian Biodiversity', 656.
8. Peter Boomgaard, 'Environmental Impact on the European Presence in Southeast Asia, 17th – 19th Centuries', 26, at http://www.raco.cat/index.php/illesimperis/article/viewFile/69206/89354.
9. Boomgaard, 'Environmental Impact', 26.
10. Francis, *Laudato Si': On Care for Our Common Home*, no. 8, at http://w2.vatican.va/content/francesco/en/encyclicals/documents/papa-francesco_20150524_enciclica-laudato-si.html.
11. See John Zizioulas, 'A Comment on Pope Francis' Encyclical Laudato Si'', at https://www.patriarchate.org/-/a-comment-on-pope-francis-encyclical-laudato-si-.
12. Francis, *Laudato Si'*, no. 25.
13. See Seán McDonagh, *Climate Change: The Challenge to All of Us*, Dublin: The Columba Press, 2006, p. 48.
14. See Pontifical Council for Justice and Peace, *Compendium of the Social Doctrine of the Church*, Cittá del Vaticano: Libreria Editrice Vaticana, 2005, no. 468.
15. See Roser and Seidel, *Climate Justice*, pp. 90, 94.
16. Jürgen Moltmann, *Ethics of Hope*, Minneapolis: Fortress Press, 2012, p. 183.
17. See Leonardo Boff, 'Respect and Care for the Community of Life with Understanding, Compassion, and Love', in Peter Blaze Corcoran (ed.), *The Earth Charter in Action: Toward a Sustainable World*, Amsterdam: KIT Publishers, 2005, p. 44.
18. *Universal Declaration of Rights of Mother Earth*, Cochabamba, Bolivia, 22 April 2010), Article 2, 1.c; at https://therightsofnature.org/universal-declaration/.
19. James LaFrankie, 'Why Native Trees?', in Marietta Marciano (ed.), *Philippine Native Trees 101: Up Close and Personal*, Quezon City: Green Convergence for Safe Food, Healthy Environment and Sustainable Economy; and Hortica Filipina, Inc., 2012, p. 309.
20. Lorraine Chow, '1.5 Million Volunteers Plant 66 Million Trees in 12 Hours, Breaking Guinness World Record', 3 July 2017, at https://www.ecowatch.com/india-trees-world-record-2452569239.html?fbclid=IwAR0HXIaY362BcfSWuBSVxhsg-0oozBlAFlVUw7QbTjxpoehXT_rkELzDdQU.
21. Section 8 of Republic Act No. 10176, at https://www.lawphil.net/statutes/repacts/ra2012/ra_10176_2012.html.

Contributors

LUKAS AVENDAÑO is an anthropologist and *muxe* performance artist, Zapotec, who presents aesthetic interventions on the political body, around topics such as gender, sexuality, and ethnic subjectivity. His choreographies: *Réquiem para un alcaraván* (2012) *No soy persona, soy mariposa* (2017) and *¿Dónde está Bruno? El mundo al revés* (2018) 'anthropology applied to staging' and have been presented at cultural festivals in Europe, the United States, and Latin America.
   Address: Apartado Postal 39, Santa Teresa de Jesús, Tehuantepec, CP. 70760. Oaxaca, México
   Email: avendanolukas@gmail.com

ANDRÉ MUSSKOPF recently became a Professor at the Department of Science of Religions at the Federal University of Juiz de Fora, in Minas Gerais, Brazil. Prior to that he worked at the Gender and Religions Program and as Chair of Theology and Gender and the Graduate Program in Theology at Faculdades EST, where he earned his Bachelor, Master and Doctorate degrees studying and writing about theology and sexual diversity.
   Address: Prof. Dr. André S. Musskopf, Universidade Federal de Juiz de For a, Department of Schience of Religion, Rua Júlio de Castilhos, 75/302, São Leopoldo, RS – Brasil 93030-240
   Email: asmusskopf@hotmail.com

SUSANNAH CORNWALL is Senior Lecturer in Constructive Theologies at the University of Exeter, UK, and Director of EXCEPT (Exeter Centre for Ethics and Practical Theology). Her books include *Theology and Sexuality* (2013), and *Un/familiar Theology: Reconceiving*

Contributors

Sex, Reproduction and Generativity (2017). She also edited *Thinking Again About Marriage: Key Theological Questions* (2016). Her current book project is a constructive theology of transgender.

Address: Dr. Susannah Cornwall, Department of Theology and Religion, University of Exeter, Amory Building, Rennes Drive, Exeter EX4 4RJ, UK

Email: S.M.Cornwall@exeter.ac.uk

MURPH MURPHY is working towards their Master of Divinity at ILIFF School of Theology in Denver, Colorado. They are a part-time spiritual community organizer working and living in Portland, Oregon. Murph focuses on building connection to self and others as a means to resist isolation, loneliness and injustice through writing, storytelling, and deep listening in North, Central, and South Americas.

Address: 1915 NE Highland St, Portland, OR 97211, USA

Email: mmurphy@iliff.edu

FR. PAUL UCHECHUKWU comes from Nigeria. He is a Catholic Priest who works with a missionary order in sub-Saharan Africa. He has a degree in Economics, Philosophy, Theology and a diploma in counselling. He is involved in Parish ministry as well as giving retreats to both religious and lay groups. He is currently pursuing a Master's degree in Biblical Studies.

Address: Fr. Paul Uchechukwu, c/o Stefanie Knauss, Theology and Religious Studies, Villanova University, 800 Lancaster University, Villanova, PA 19085, USA

Email: stefanie.knauss@gmail.com

GWYNN KESSLER is Associate Professor in the Religion Department at Swarthmore College. She is the author of *Conceiving Israel: The Fetus in Rabbinic Narratives* (2009) and is currently completing her second monograph, *The Crooked and The Straight: Queer Theory and Rabbinic Literature*. Address: Prof. Dr. Gwynn Kessler, Department of Religion, Swarthmore College, 500 College Ave, 208 Pearson Hall, Swarthmore, PA 19081, USA

Email: gkessle1@swarthmore.edu

CARMENMARGARITA SÁNCHEZ DE LEÓN is an ordained minister

Contributors

of the Universal Fraternity of Metropolitan Community Churches. She is a professor in the Mexican Theological Community. Her special interests are queer theology, feminist theologies and human rights.
  Address: Rubens 46, Colonia San Juan., Delegación Benito Juárez, CP 03730. Ciudad de México, Mexico
  Email: revmargaritasanchezdeleon@mccchurch.net

SHARON A. BONG is Associate Professor of Gender Studies at the School of Arts and Social Sciences, Monash University Malaysia. She has authored *The Tension Between Women's Rights and Religions: The Case of Malaysia* (2006) and edited *Trauma, Memory and Transformation in Southeast Asia* (2014). She is currently consultant to and former coordinator of the Ecclesia of Women in Asia and a forum writer for the Catholic Theological Ethics in the World Church.
  Address: Associate Prof. Dr. Sharon A. Bong, School of Arts & Social Sciences, Monash University Malaysia, Jalan Lagoon Selatan, 47500 Bandar Sunway, Selangor Darul Ehsan, Malaysia
  Email: Sharon.bong@monash.edu

NONTANDO HADEBE is a lay Catholic woman theologian and Research Fellow in Faculty of Theology and Religion, University of the Free State (Bloemfontein, South Africa) and part-time lecturer at St Augustine College of South Africa. With Ezra Chitandao, she edited *Compassionate Circles: African Women Theologians Facing HIV* (2009). She has written on gender, trinitarian theology, ecology, HIV/AIDS, LGBTIQ and decoloniality, and presents a weekly radio program on Radio Veritas.
  Address: Dr. Nontando Hadebe, St Augustine College, 53 Ley Road, Victory Park, Johannesburg, 2195, South Africa
  Email: noehadebe@gmail.com

ÁNGEL F. MÉNDEZ MONTOYA - the author is a professor and researcher in the departments of religious studies, philosophy, humanities and the doctoral programme in critical gender studies in the Universidad Iberoamericana in Mexico City. Among many other articles and anthologies, he is the author of *The Theology of Food: Eating and the Eucharist* (2009).
  Address: Universidad Iberoamericana, Departamento de Ciencias Religiosas, Prol. Paseo de la Reforma 880, Lomas de Santa Fe, C.P. 01219,

Contributors

Ciudad de México, Mexico
Email: angel.mendez@ibero.mx

MARILÚ ROJAS SALAZAR holds a doctorate in systematic theology from the Catholic University of Louvain. Currently she is tenured professor of theology at the Universidad Iberoamericana in Mexico City, directs the doctorate in Critical Gender Studies at the same university. She is the editor of the journal *Sophias*, an interdisciplinary journal of feminist theology. Her recent publications include: *Incorporación de la Reflexión Teológico Feminista como uno de los retos de la academia teológica en México* (2018), Alberto Anguiano García & Julián Arturo López Amozorrutia (Co eds.) *Pensar a Dios desde este Lado del Muro* (México: Universidad Pontificia de México, 2018), 97-115, and *Decolonizing Theology: Panentheist Spiritualities and Proposals from the Ecofeminist Epistemologies of the South* (2018).

Address: Dr. Marilú Rojas Salazar, Avenida Erasmo Castellanos Quinto 224, Col. Educación. Del. Coyoacán, CP. 04400 Ciudad de México, Mexico
Email: Saroma24@gmail.com

GERALD O. WEST is Professor of Old Testament/Hebrew Bible and African Biblical Hermeneutics in the School of Religion, Philosophy, and Classics at the University of KwaZulu-Natal, South Africa. He is also Director of the Ujamaa Centre for Community Development and Research, a project in which socially engaged biblical scholars and ordinary African readers of the Bible from poor, working-class, and marginalised communities collaborate for social transformation.

CHARLENE VAN DER WALT is an Associate Professor and Head of Gender and Religion programme in the School of Religion, Philosophy, and Classics at the University of KwaZulu-Natal. She is also responsible for the Body Theology work done within the Ujamaa Centre for Community Development and Research.

Address: Prof. Gerald West/Prof. Charlene van der Walt, School of Religion, Philosophy, and Classics, University of KwaZulu-Natal, Private Bag X01, Scottsville, 3209, South Africa
Email: west@ukzn.ac.za / vanderwaltc@ukzn.ac.za

Contributors

SHANON SHAH is Lecturer in Religion and Social Science at King's College London. His research explores the boundary between marginal and mainstream movements in contemporary Islam and Christianity, specifically through the lens of gender and sexuality. He is the author of *The Making of a Gay Muslim: Religion, Sexuality and Identity in Malaysia and Britain* (2018) and is a deputy editor of *Critical Muslim*.
   Address: Dr Shanon Shah, Theology and Religious Studies, Virginia Woolf Building, King's College London, 22 Kingsway, London WC2B 6NR, UK
   Email: shanonshah@gmail.com

CONRADO ZEPEDA MIRAMONTES is a Mexican Jesuit, with a Bachelor's degree in philosophy, social sciences and theology, and a Master's in Social Anthropology. For more than thirty years he has worked with vulnerable groups: indigenous people, young people on the streets and with addictions. Since 2016 he has been working with migrants and refugees. He is a member of the Jesuit Migrant and Refugee Services in Mexico.

REYNALDO D. RALUTO is a Roman Catholic priest of the Diocese of Malaybalay (Philippines). He holds a licentiate and doctorate in theology from the Catholic University of Leuven (Belgium). He serves as Academic Dean of St. John Vianney Theological Seminary in Cagayan de Oro. His recent publications include *Poverty and Ecology at the Crossroads* (2015).
   Address: Prof. Dr. Reynaldo D. Raluto, St. John Vianney Theological Seminary, Camaman-an, 9000 Cagayan de Oro, The Philippines
   Email: reyrals@yahoo.com

CONCILIUM
International Journal of Theology

FOUNDERS
Anton van den Boogaard; Paul Brand; Yves Congar, OP; Hans Küng; Johann Baptist Metz; Karl Rahner, SJ; Edward Schillebeeckx

BOARD OF DIRECTORS
President: Thierry-Marie Courau OP
Vice-Presidents: Linda Hogan and Daniel Franklin Pilario CM

BOARD OF EDITORS
Susan Abraham, Los Angeles (USA)
Michel Andraos, Chicago (USA)
Mile Babic' OFM, Sarajevo (Bosna i Hercegovina)
Antony John Baptist, Bangalore (India)
Michelle Becka, Würzburg (Deutschland)
Bernadeth Caero Bustillos, Osnabrück (Deutschland)
Catherine Cornille, Boston (USA)
Thierry-Marie Courau OP, Paris (France)
Geraldo Luiz De Mori SJ, Belo Horizonte (Brasil)
Enrico Galavotti, Chieti (Italia)
Margareta Gruber OSF, Vallendar (Deutschland)
Linda Hogan, Dublin (Ireland)
Huang Po-Ho, Tainan (Zhōnghuá Mínguó)
Stefanie Knauss, Villanova (USA)
Carlos Mendoza-Álvarez OP, Ciudad de México (México)
Gianluca Montaldi FN, Brescia (Italia)
Agbonkhianmeghe Orobator SJ, Nairobi (Kenya)
Daniel Franklin Pilario CM, Quezon City (Filipinas)
Léonard Santedi Kinkupu, Kinshasa (RD Congo)
João J. Vila-Chã SJ, Roma (Italia)

PUBLISHERS
SCM Press (London, UK)
Matthias-Grünewald Verlag (Ostfildern, Germany)
Editrice Queriniana (Brescia, Italy)
Editorial Verbo Divino (Estella, Spain)
EditoraVozes (Petropolis, Brazil)

Concilium Secretariat:
Couvent de l'Annonciation
222 rue du Faubourg Saint-Honoré
75008 – Paris (France)
secretariat.concilium@gmail.com
Executive secretary: Gianluca Montaldi FN

http://www.concilium.in

The Canterbury Dictionary of HYMNOLOGY The result of over ten years of research by an international team of editors, The Canterbury Dictionary of Hymnology is the major online reference work on hymns, hymn-writers and traditions.
www.hymnology.co.uk

CHURCH TIMES The Church Times, founded in 1863, has become the world's leading Anglican newspaper. It offers professional reporting of UK and international church news, in-depth features on faith, arts and culture, wide-ranging comment and all the latest clergy jobs. Available in print and online.
www.churchtimes.co.uk

Crucible Crucible is the Christian journal of social ethics. It is produced quarterly, pulling together some of the best practitioners, thinkers, and theologians in the field. Each issue reflects theologically on a key theme of political, social, cultural, or environmental significance.
www.cruciblejournal.co.uk

JLS Joint Liturgical Studies offers a valuable contribution to the study of liturgy. Each issue considers a particular aspect of liturgical development, such as the origins of the Roman rite, Anglican Orders, welcoming the Baptised, and Anglican Missals.
www.jointliturgicalstudies.co.uk

magnet Magnet is a resource magazine published three times a year. Packed with ideas for worship, inspiring artwork and stories of faith and justice from around the world.
www.ourmagnet.co.uk

For more information on these publications visit the websites listed above or contact **Hymns Ancient & Modern:**
Tel.: +44 (0)1603 785 910
**Write to: Subscriptions, Hymns Ancient & Modern,
13a Hellesdon Park Road, Norwich NR6 5DR**

Concilium Subscription Information

February   2020/1: *Contextual Theologies Facing the Challenge of Global Violence*

April   2020/2: *Masculinities*

July   2020/3: *Theology, Power and Governance*

October   2020/4: *Signs of Hope for Muslim-Christian Dialogue*

New subscribers: to receive the next five issues of Concilium please copy this form, complete it in block capitals and send it with your payment to the address below. Alternatively subscribe online at www.conciliumjournal.co.uk

Please enter my annual subscription for Concilium starting with issue 2019/5.

Individuals
____ £52 UK
____ £75 overseas and (Euro €92, US $110)

Institutions
____ £75 UK
____ £95 overseas and (Euro €120, US $145)

Postage included – airmail for overseas subscribers

Payment Details:
Payment can be made by cheque (£ Sterling only), by credit/debit card or bank transfer.
a. I enclose a cheque for £ _____ Payable to Hymns Ancient and Modern Ltd
b. To pay by Visa/Mastercard please contact us on +44(0)1603 785911 or go to www.conciliumjournal.co.uk
c. To pay in US $ or Euro € by bank transfer please contact us on +44(0)1603 785911

Contact Details:
Name ....
Address ....
....
Telephone .... E-mail ....

Send your order to *Concilium,* **Hymns Ancient and Modern Ltd**
13a Hellesdon Park Road, Norwich NR6 5DR, UK
E-mail: concilium@hymnsam.co.uk
or order online at www.conciliumjournal.co.uk

Customer service information
All orders must be prepaid. Your subscription will begin with the next issue of Concilium. If you have any queries or require Information about other payment methods, please contact our Customer Services department.